SHAW

Smith, Emily Esfahani.
Shaw in an hour

DEC 0 8 2011

BY EMILY ESFAHANI SMITH

SUSAN C. MOORE, SERIES EDITOR

PLAYWRIGHTS in an hour
know the playwright, love the play

IN AN HOUR BOOKS • HANOVER, NEW HAMPSHIRE • INANHOURBOOKS.COM
AN IMPRINT OF SMITH AND KRAUS PUBLISHERS, INC • SMITHANDKRAUS.COM

*With grateful thanks to Carl R. Mueller, whose
fascinating introductions to his translations of
the Greek and German playwrights provided
inspiration for this series.*

Published by In an Hour Books
an imprint of Smith and Kraus, Inc.
177 Lyme Road, Hanover, NH 03755
inanhourbooks.com SmithandKraus.com

Know the playwright, love the play.

In an Hour, In a Minute, and Theater IQ are registered trademarks of
In an Hour Books.

Front cover design by Dan Mehling, dmehling@gmail.com
Text design by Kate Mueller, Electric Dragon Productions
Book production by Dede Cummings Design, DCDesign@sover.net

ISBN-13: 978-1-936232-24-6
ISBN-10: 1-936232-24-3
Library of Congress Control Number: 2009943219

CONTENTS

Why Playwrights in an Hour?

This new series by Smith and Kraus Publishers titled Playwrights in an Hour has a dual purpose for being: one academic, the other general. For the general reader, this volume, as well as the many others in the series, offers in compact form the information needed for a basic understanding and appreciation of the works of each volume's featured playwright. Which is not to say that there don't exist volumes on end devoted to each playwright under consideration. But inasmuch as few are blessed with enough time to read the splendid scholarship that is available, a brief, highly focused accounting of the playwright's life and work is in order. The central feature of the series, a thirty- to forty-page essay, integrates the playwright into the context of his or her time and place. The volumes, though written to high standards of academic integrity, are accessible in style and approach to the general reader as well as to the student and, of course, to the theater professional and theatergoer. These books will serve for the brushing up of one's knowledge of a playwright's career, to the benefit of theater work or theatergoing. The Playwrights in an Hour series represents all periods of Western theater: Aeschylus to Shakespeare to Wedekind to Ibsen to Williams to Beckett, and on to the great contemporary playwrights who continue to offer joy and enlightenment to a grateful world.

Carl R. Mueller
School of Theater, Film and Television
Department of Theater
University of California, Los Angeles

Introduction

G eorge Bernard Shaw in an hour? It usually takes an hour just for him to clear his throat. Shaw is a writer who doesn't simply compose a play, he builds an entire social, political, religious, and philosophical framework around it. Scorning the role of "mere" artist in favor of his preferred function of "artist-philosopher," Shaw invariably offers discourses not just on the subject of his play, but on the conduct of humanity, the state of society, and the nature of the universe. Ann Whitfield's concluding line in *Man and Superman,* "Go on talking, Jack," is clearly Shaw's self-mocking recognition of his own incorrigible loquacity.

Can such an inveterate rhetorician be listed among the great dramatic artists? Was Shaw a poet or — like Eugene O'Neill — a man who simply had the makings of one? That question continues to be debated despite the fact that few of his illustrious Irish contemporaries — neither James Joyce, nor Oscar Wilde, nor W. B. Yeats — held Shaw in more than mild esteem (indeed, Yeats dismissed him as the chosen author of very clever journalists). Still, at least one major artist, T. S. Eliot, recognized there was a poet in Bernard Shaw, that is, "until he was born — and the poet in Shaw was stillborn."

Eliot was suggesting that Shaw's poetic nature was often crippled by his intrusive intellect, and even more by his odd incapacity to see the darker corners of human nature. (That role he gave to the Devil in *Man and Superman.*) Shaw's blindness to evil may explain why he was still praising Hitler and Mussolini long after those dictators began pursuing less salubrious goals than making the trains run on time. Shaw rejected Darwin for similar reasons. Shaw simply could not contemplate an arbitrary and indifferent natural system that "banished mind from the universe." In place of Darwin's evolutionary theories he substituted Lamarck's crackpot ideas about creative evolution. And although Shaw was among the first to recognize the importance of Henrik Ibsen, Shaw's early study of him, *The Quintessence of Ibsenism,* transformed that radical anarchist into a species of domesticated social worker, not unlike Shaw's own Andrew Undershaft building comfortable Levittowns for homeless workers in *Major Barbara.*

On the other hand, it is undeniable that Shaw wrote some really sublime plays. His most tragic and pessimistic work, *Heartbreak House,* found its genesis in Shaw's despair over World War I (Shaw delayed the play's debut until the war was over). It was a play in which Shaw for a moment stopped grinning in order to study and diagnose the deteriorating condition of man. The result was an apocalyptic fantasy that not only faulted human institutions, but the nature of humankind itself, with an eloquence that went much deeper than reason. In *Heartbreak House,* the poet in Shaw is no longer stillborn; he is completely functional and working at full strength.

Shaw also wrote a number of excellent social comedies with philosophical overtones, among them *Pygmalion, Man and Superman,* and *Major Barbara.* These, and others, are genuine contributions to dramatic literature. But while we value Shaw's ruminations on the life force, creative evolution, the superman, phonetics, eugenics, and other passing concerns, we value even more the intelligence, eloquence, and intensity with which Shaw expressed those ideas.

Will Shaw's plays, like the ideas he was preoccupied with, begin to fade, or will they survive as penetrating works of art, despite their obsolescent view of humankind? There is no question his plays will always endure as lively artifacts of Victorian comedy; but the final judgment on whether they are more than that has yet to be made. For the moment, he still holds our attention with his wonderful surface brilliance.

Robert Brustein
Founding Director of the Yale and American Repertory Theatres,
Distinguished Scholar in Residence, Suffolk University
Senior Research Fellow, Harvard University

SHAW

IN A MINUTE

AGE	DATE	
—	**1856**	Enter George Bernard Shaw "fifty years too soon," as he would later say.
3	1859	Charles Dickens publishes *A Tale of Two Cities*.
8	1864	"In God We Trust" first appears on U.S. coins.
12	1868	Disraeli becomes British prime minister and resigns the same year.
15	1871	British parliament legalizes labor unions.
21	1877	Henrik Ibsen publishes *The Pillars of Society*.
25	1881	Political parties are founded in Japan.
35	**1891**	**George Bernard Shaw — *The Quintessence of Ibsenism* published**
40	1896	First modern Olympics held in Athens.
43	1899	Oscar Wilde publishes *The Importance of Being Earnest*.
46	**1902**	**George Bernard Shaw — *Mrs. Warren's Profession* published**
47	1903	The Alaskan frontier is settled.
48	1904	Anton Chekhov publishes *The Cherry Orchard*.
49	**1905**	**George Bernard Shaw — *Man and Superman* published**
50	1906	Night shift for women internationally forbidden.
55	1911	Archibald Henderson publishes *Shaw: His Life and Works*.
56	1912	Major labor disputes disrupt streets of London.
60	**1916**	**George Bernard Shaw — *Pygmalion* published**
61	**1917**	**Shaw writes that the Russian Revolution was a "triumph."**
63	**1919**	**George Bernard Shaw — *Heartbreak House* published**
64	1920	W. B. Yeats writes "The Second Coming."
65	1921	D. H. Lawrence publishes *Women in Love*.
71	1927	Babe Ruth hits sixty home runs for the Yankees.
76	1932	Amelia Earhart is the first woman to fly alone across the Atlantic.
80	1936	Civil war erupts in Spain.
82	1938	Hitler's troops march into Austria.
84	1940	"You Are My Sunshine" is hit song in the United States.
87	1943	Penicillin era begins.
93	1949	George Orwell publishes *Nineteen Eighty-Four*.
94	**1950**	**Exit George Bernard Shaw.**

A snapshot of the playwright's world. From historical events to pop-culture and the literary landscape of the time, this brief list catalogues events that directly or indirectly impacted the playwright's writing.

Shaw

HIS WORKS

DRAMA

Plays Unpleasant

        Widowers' Houses

        Mrs. Warren's Profession

        The Philanderer

Plays Pleasant

        Arms and the Man

        Candida

        The Man of Destiny

Three Plays for Puritans

        The Devil's Disciple

        Caesar and Cleopatra

        Captain Brassbound's Conversion

The Admirable Bashville

Man and Superman

John Bull's Other Island

How He Lied to Her Husband

Major Barbara

The Doctor's Dilemma

Getting Married

The Fascinating Foundling

The Glimpse of Reality

Press Cuttings

The Shewing Up of Blanco Posnet

Misalliance

The Dark Lady of the Sonnets

Fanny's First Play

This section presents a complete list of the playwright's works in chronological order.

NOVELS

SHORT STORIES

"The Miraculous Revenge"

"The Black Girl in Search of God"

ESSAYS

"Quintessence of Ibsenism"

"The Perfect Wagnerite, Commentary on the Ring"

"Maxims for Revolutionists"

"How to Write a Popular Play"

"Treatise on Parents and Children"

"Common Sense About the War"

"The Intelligent Woman's Guide to Socialism and Capitalism"

"Dictators: Let Us Have More of Them"

Onstage with Shaw

Introducing Colleagues and Contemporaries
of George Bernard Shaw

 THEATER

Antonin Artaud, French playwright
Henry Irving, English theater director
Richard Mansfield, American actor
Sean O'Casey, Irish playwright
Luigi Pirandello, Italian playwright
Ellen Terry, English actress
Frank Wedekind, German playwright
Oscar Wilde, Irish playwright

 ARTS

Claude Debussy, French composer
Edgar Degas, French painter
Isadora Duncan, American dancer
Edvard Munch, Norwegian painter
Pablo Picasso, Spanish painter
Auguste Rodin, French sculptor
Igor Stravinsky, Russian composer
Giuseppe Verdi, Italian composer

 FILM

Charlie Chaplin, English actor
Clark Gable, American actor
Greta Garbo, Swedish actress
Audrey Hepburn, British actress
Alfred Hitchcock, English filmmaker

This section lists contemporaries whom the playwright may or may not have known.

Giovonni Pastrone, Italian film director

George Albert Smith, English pioneer of cinema

Shirley Temple, American actress

POLITICS/MILITARY

Winston Churchill, prime minister of England

Alfred Dreyfus, French army officer

Dwight D. Eisenhower, American president and general

Hermann Goering, Nazi leader

Chiang Kai-shek, Chinese general and statesman

Henry Morgenthau Jr., American statesman

Leon Trotsky, Russian-Ukrainian Bolshevik

Chaim Weizmann, first president of Israel

SCIENCE

Louis de Broglie, French physicist

Thomas Edison, American inventor

Albert Einstein, German-born American physicist

Sigmund Freud, Austrian psychologist

E. P. Hubble, American astronomer

Carl Jung, Swiss psychologist

Ernest Rutherford, English scientist

Richard von Krafft-Ebing, German neurologist

LITERATURE

Joseph Conrad, English novelist

Fyodor Dostoevsky, Russian novelist

A. E. Housman, English poet

James Joyce, Irish novelist

Franz Kafka, Austrian-Czech novelist

D. H. Lawrence, English novelist and poet

Rainer Maria Rilke, Austrian poet

Emile Zola, French novelist

RELIGION/PHILOSOPHY

Henri Bergson, French philosopher

John Dewey, American philosopher

William James, American philosopher

Vladimir Lenin, Russian political scientist

Bertrand Russell, English philosopher

Oswald Spengler, German philosopher

Booker T. Washington, American thinker, educator, political
leader, author

Max Weber, German sociologist

SPORTS

Ty Cobb, American baseball player

Pierre de Coubertin, French founder of modern Olympics

Jack Dempsey, American boxer

Suzanne Lenglen, French tennis player

Sugar Ray Robinson, American boxer

Jim Thorpe, American Olympic athlete

Mildred Ella ("Babe") Didrikson Zaharias, American golfer

Satchel Paige, American baseball player

INDUSTRY/BUSINESS

Lord Beaverbrook, Canadian-British business tycoon

Andrew Carnegie, Scottish-American industrialist and
philanthropist

Henry Ford, American industrialist

Conrad Hilton, American hotelier

J. P Morgan, American financier and banker

William Randoph Hearst, American newspaper publisher

John D. Rockefeller, American oil tycoon

Adolph Zukor, Hungarian-American film mogul

SHAW

in an
hour

INTRODUCTION

The mystic fog of the Emerald Isle was illuminated for a time by the brilliance of W. B. Yeats, Oscar Wilde, Sydney Gurdy, and George Bernard Shaw. Shaw was by far the most eminent of these four prominent Irishmen.

Time and circumstance perhaps inform Shaw's biography more than anything. Shaw grappled with his individualism and with the society that sought to undermine it. He would write and rewrite history in his plays, while allowing his readers a somewhat obstructed view into his conscience. Often, history and conscience clashed, but Shaw rejoiced in paradox. In this way he reconciled different strands within himself, and he did so by assuming the role of a reformer. As a social reformer, he was a Fabian, which in the context of the day was a rather conservative stripe of socialism. As a reformer of the human soul, he reached well into the human conscience, often criticizing it in its current condition while offering some hope in the promise of progress. He was a realist, but both psychologically and politically he

This is the core of the book. The essay places the playwright in the context of his or her world and analyzes the influences and inspirations within that world.

was optimistic about the potential of humanity and society — to the point that his realism bled over into idealism, a paradox indeed. And yet, his bleak family life, his experience with impoverished London, and his having to endure two world wars required him to cope with reality with a dash of hope and an aside of humor. This stunted reality is what Shaw explores in his plays.

HISTORY AND SOCIETAL CONTEXT

George Bernard Shaw lived through the seeming stability of the Victorian era into the shaky uncertainty of the modern world. He was born on July 26, 1856, and died in 1950, living through the horror of World War I and World War II. His life was filled with major social convulsions: Mass manufacturing produced mass consumerism in those years. With the Industrial Revolution and the advance of commercialization, the Western world was becoming a mechanistic assembly line. This gave rise to a witch's brew of Marxism and social Darwinism, Freud and Nietzsche. Metaphysical systems, which had once explained the world, buckled in the face of materialism and empiricism. The world was becoming more secular. Even art could be explained in terms of evolution and natural selection, casting religion and transcendence aside. Notably, the Naturalism movement in theater and literature, influenced by Darwin, examined how the environment and heredity determine character and behavior.

Victorian morality tried either to constrain or to ignore this new amoral worldview that was assaulting tradition and everything good, decent, and civil. But to Shaw, the moral code of Victorian Britain was empty at best and hypocritical at worst, and he sought to expose its fallacies in his plays. If Victorian society could simultaneously pro-duce a complacent landed aristocracy and a destitute pauper class that lived in tenements, then something was flawed in the way society organized itself.

Shaw was interested in exposing the individual's blind acceptance of society's arbitrary and harmful moral strictures. He further exposed his characters as idiotic sentimentalists for accepting Victorian ideals that were in no way grounded in reality. Michael Holroyd quotes Shaw in his excellent biography of the playwright: "English decency is a . . . string of taboos. You must not mention this; you must not appear conscious of that . . . everything that must not be mentioned in public is mentioned in private as a naughty joke." Shaw's merciless exposure of such absurdity often produced unease in his audience. Audience members were now forced to question — some of them for the first time in their lives — their devotion to what Shaw saw as a flawed social structure.

With the advent of World War I in 1914, Shaw professed a determined pacifism that put people off. His "Common Sense About the War," an article written for *The New York Times* in 1914, earned him the epithet "Most Hated Man in England," and he went so far as to assert that the British were as pugnacious as the Germans.

The war provided Shaw and other like-minded socialists with a stark example of capitalism's fatal flaws. Many reformers understood the war as the inevitable consequence of the Victorian era's societal problems coupled with industrialization. To them, industrialization, nationalization, commercialization, and romantic militarism led to the evil of World War I. For Shaw, the unequal distribution of wealth throughout Europe caused the war. Distribute the wealth equitably, Shaw reasoned, and peace would soon follow.

The political climate was buzzing — thanks to Shaw and those like him who, in turn, were influenced by Marx and Hegel. In the aftermath of World War I, the middle class began to expect fast social change. The hope was that socialism would be universally implemented, replacing the flawed social structures that existed before the war. But those expectations went unrealized. Postwar Europe was greeted by the iron fists of totalitarianism and a second "final" war: World War II.

Shaw's belief that government could equitably distribute wealth and labor under the guidance of a strong socialist leader initially caused him to admire fascists and support totalitarianism. As Holroyd quotes Shaw, "All dictators begin as reformers . . . I applauded both Hitler and Mussolini while they were still in their reform phase." As it became clear that Stalin's social experiment, when taken to its rational conclusion, ended in the gulag, Shaw modified his optimism and told a friend not to expect paradise with social reconstruction. As Holroyd notes in his biography of Shaw, moves like this impelled the Fabian Beatrice Webb, a close friend and sometime antagonist of Shaw, to note in her diary, "[H]e preaches a curiously abstract utopia, which eludes criticism because of its very unreality."

Shaw lived to see the pages of the complacent Victorian era turned over to a steely modern era — an old world transitioning into the new one. The enormity of such a transition, and the opportunity to witness it, gave Shaw the material to produce a vast body of plays. Shaw needed to only look out his window or into the newspaper and he found the inspiration to create. Seeing that problems existed in the world, Shaw traced the origin of those problems back to society, as opposed to man. He wrote plays about society's problems and offered solutions in his plays. Filled with allegories and ideas, Shaw's plays were meant to teach society how to heal itself.

CHILDHOOD

Shaw's father, George Carr Shaw, was a civil servant who later became an unsuccessful wholesale grain dealer. He was a simple man whose life spun around his addictions to alcohol and money. His father's alcoholism, Shaw thought, was conditioned by a society out of which George Carr Shaw was trying to escape.

Shaw's father was a remote figure in his childhood. His detachment was outdone by his wife's bitterness toward him, which she evidenced by maintaining an icy distance from her husband and children.

Shaw's mother, Lucinda Gurly Shaw, was the daughter of a poor landowner and sixteen years younger than her husband. A semiprofessional singer with musical ambitions, she was miserable with the lot she was handed and made her misery painfully apparent to her children by neglecting them. But Shaw desperately needed the affections of his mother. When he dreamt of his mother as a child, she was always his wife and his mother simultaneously, which in no way seemed incestuous to Shaw. Indeed, many of his most potent images and ideas belonged to an abstract world unrealizable in the actual world. His dreams often evolved into his plays. For example, his most philosophical play, *Man and Superman*, takes place in a dream world.

As a child, Shaw found refuge within the pages of books: Macaulay, Eliot, Shakespeare, Dickens, and Mill. Shaw read a great deal. Indeed, he replaced the time he would have spent at a university, had he gone, with the time he spent in the library. Only in the world of books did Shaw's imagination truly come alive. Shaw learned to make a loveless childhood less painful with his active imagination. He wrote in the preface to *Immaturity* that he felt at home only in his imagination: "[A]ll my life I was a sojourner on this planet rather than a native of it . . . I was at home only in the realm of my imagination, and at my ease only with the mighty dead." In his lost childhood, Shaw's philosophy was conceived: He reached out for new worlds, wondrous possibilities, infinite potentials.

Other components of Shaw's philosophy sparked in his early youth were humor and paradox. Shaw was a mischievous and lighthearted boy who tried to forge comedy out of the loneliness of his childhood. This transformation can be seen in Shaw's reaction to the death of his aunt Ellen, whose hunched back was offset by a pretty face. Shaw's imagination turned her into an enchantress. Upon learning of her death, Shaw remembers crying and experiencing the terrifying fear that his grief would last forever. Later, he would consider such sadness taboo and claim, as Holroyd quotes Shaw, that "people who cry and grieve never remember. I never grieve and never forget." He cast aside sadness and "laughed pain out of existence." Shaw's childhood impulse to put laughter where tears should be, shielding his vulnerability, would develop into the cool, measured, and detached quality that was characteristic of the adult Shaw.

Growing up in a household where there was neither hate nor love meant that there was also no guidance or mentoring. As a result of the neglect and indifference he experienced at the hands of his parents, Shaw became excessively self-sufficient and independent. When faced with a dilemma for which most people would seek advice, Shaw turned inward, into the wisdom of his own mind. He trusted only the legitimacy of his own instincts. It is no wonder, then, that he gave his friends the advice, "Always strive to find out what to do by thinking, without asking anybody," as Holroyd points out. Shaw trusted his own instincts before anyone else's — for good reason. After all, it worked.

On the other hand, his independence mingled with his politics and philosophy as well. His parents — who were meant to love him, guide him, and keep him safe — ignored him. And so he disdained all authorities in general, except the authority of his own mind. He was always the leader, the patrician, the lecturer, the playwright, the director — in short, the center of attention. He desperately sought to replace that which he never received. Naturally, this caused not a little bit of self-conscious conceitedness, which may be best seen when he compares himself to one of the greatest geniuses ever written into dramatic existence: "like Hamlet I lack ambition and its push," as he notes in his diary.

Thus, when Shaw addressed a human problem, rather than categorizing it as emotional or psychological, he would place it in the realm of politics and ideas so as to distance himself from pain. Emotional vulnerability was often so draining for Shaw that he chose instead to immerse himself in the sterile waters of economics, politics, and history. In his works and words, Shaw chose concepts rather than emotions to fill the void of a silent, loveless childhood home.

THE MOVE TO LONDON

When Shaw was sixteen years old, his mother left his father and traveled to London with her voice teacher and paramour, George Vandeleur Lee, to pursue a musical career. She took with her Shaw's two older half sisters, Lucinda Frances, also a singer, and Elinor Agnes. Four years later, in 1876, Shaw joined his mother and sisters and lived with them for nine years in London.

Shaw launched his writing career during these years. He ghost-wrote Lee's music column for the London *Hornet* and frequented the British Museum and public libraries, where he assiduously read and studied. He began writing and submitting essays, articles, and poems to local publications, but most of his writing was rejected, including five novels. He finally found his niche writing musical and dramatic criticism.

Shaw's avid reading, particularly of Marx's *Das Kapital* in 1883, deeply influenced his thinking about economics. Shaw became a committed socialist and even declared himself a communist much later in his life (in the 1930s). To Shaw, as Holroyd quotes, socialism was "a state of society in which the entire income of the country is divided between all the people in exactly equal shares, without regard to their industry, their character, or any other consideration except the consideration that they are living human beings . . . that is Socialism and nothing else is Socialism."

In Victorian London, at that time the richest city in the world, financial stature was all — and Shaw had none when he arrived as a young man. By contrast, his fellow Irishman and dandy extraordinaire Oscar Wilde came straight from Dublin's fashionable Merrion Square to London's fashionable West End by way of Trinity College, Dublin, then Magdalene College, Oxford. Like Wilde, Shaw's opposition to Victorianism took the form of a socialism that attempted to unite art and politics, specifically by wedding art with socialism. However, while Wilde opposed the Victorians on moral and artistic grounds, Shaw undermined Victoria and her era with an economic argument. Determined to oppose social inequality boldly, Shaw declared himself, in his diaries, a "Socialist, an Atheist, and a Vegetarian." Clearly, Shaw required a cause to live for to fill an emptiness that had been plaguing him since his youth.

FABIAN SOCIALISM

Shaw found the Fabian Society of London compatible with his unique brand of conservative socialism, and he joined the society in 1884. Sydney and Beatrice Webb, who ran the society, would be friends with Shaw to the end of their days. The tenets of Fabianism included a standard commitment to socialism that expressed itself through a reasoned voice, pragmatic solutions, popular democracy, and the belief that society must, at all costs, be safeguarded against a revolution.

Shaw thrived among the Fabians, and he used his speaking and writing talents to give mundane socialism an artistic shine. Through Shaw's connections with the press — *The World, The Star, The Pall Mall Gazette*, to name just a few publications — he was able to propagandize for the society. Writing under the pseudonym Corno di Bassetto for *The Star*, Shaw managed to weave Fabian doctrines even into his music criticism. He popularized the dogmas and ideals in which he and the Fabians believed. As Holroyd notes, Shaw wrote that "[a]ll great art and literature is propaganda," and Shaw esteemed journalism as the greatest form of literary expression.

Growing up in Dublin, Shaw was struck by the destitution in the Dublin slums he knew well. His goal was to abolish what he called white slavery. To Shaw, poverty itself was the ultimate evil of the world, and he located its source in the body of society. Since society tolerated the virus of evil, society needed a cure. For Shaw, evil was not a matter of personal choice but a by-product of institutions. In 1886, when Shaw was thirty, London, with its filthy tenement houses, its women driven to prostitution, and its children dying of tuberculosis, put a human face on an ideological problem for Shaw. These factors solidified Shaw's commitment to socialism and caused him to indict laissez-faire capitalism as the root of society's evil.

When 30 percent of the population was living in squalor in the richest city in the world, what else but capitalism could be the cause? Since capitalism explained the wealth, then, in the mind of Shaw, it must also explain the poverty. Shaw concluded that the current distribution of wealth was based on class rather than on merit or talent. He believed that artificial and arbitrary class barriers needed to be abolished. Once class was abolished and rendered meaningless, the happiness of humanity would be ensured by evenly distributing the wealth generated by society. Land ownership would be nationalized since human nature was pristine and incapable of greed and cruelty. The masses of men that compose society would work together to contribute to an abstract common good that ensured the greatest amount of happiness for the greatest number of men.

SHAW IN LOVE

Although Shaw most often turned to politics to fill his emptiness, he occasionally found relief under Cupid's spell, which first hit him in February 1882 when he made the acquaintance of Alice Lockett, his first serious girlfriend. His relationship with Lockett reveals how Shaw-the-Reformer often butted heads with Shaw-the-Man. Lockett was determined to rise in society, and Shaw was determined to relieve her of her dreams. The ramped-up socialist in him wanted to reform everything that he came in contact with. He took on Lockett as another of his ideological projects, and he lectured her rather than loved her, berated rather than praised her. Though Lockett resented such treatment, she did possess the necessary qualities to compel Shaw to fall deeply in love with her. He, in turn, wanted to inspire love in Lockett — as he would with many other women.

Among his many women was Jenny Patterson, with whom Shaw became involved at age twenty-nine and to whom he lost his virginity. This tempestuous relationship lasted until 1893. While still involved with Patterson, he took up with fellow socialist Grace Black and with actress Florence Farr. Shaw also became involved with May Morris, daughter of the Pre-Raphaelite artist and designer William Morris. Morris' involvement with Shaw led to the break up of her marriage to Henry Halliday Sparling, secretary of the Socialist League. Reputedly, Morris had hoped Shaw would marry her after her marriage with Sparling ended. One of Shaw's most famous platonic involvements was with actress Mrs. Patrick Campbell, with whom he maintained a nearly forty-year correspondence of ardent letters and for whom he wrote the part of Eliza in *Pygmalion*.

In 1885, Shaw began a correspondence with another actress, Ellen Terry, who was nine years older than he. Over the course of their correspondence, the two fell in love but did not meet until much later. By not meeting, Shaw created an idealized relationship between himself and Terry in which both played the role of lovers. They didn't realize the fiction of their love in the real world: Ellen was married, after all. An unexpected sentimentalism is exposed here in Shaw: He did not want to meet Ellen Terry because he preferred to contain her in his imagination, where he was always at home. As Holroyd quotes Shaw: "I, too, fear to break the spell, remorses, presentiments, all sorts of tendernesses wring my heart at the thought of materializing this beautiful friendship of ours by a meeting."

Shaw in love is Shaw at his most vulnerable, and some of his most touching prose is captured in letters he wrote to his lovers, some of which Holroyd reproduces in his biography of the playwright: "[W]e are too cautious, too calculating, too selfish, too heartless, to venture head over heel in love," he warned Lockett, and yet he did fall in love with one woman after another. In any case, one sure way for Shaw to avoid the disarming charms of a woman was to occupy himself with other matters in his mind of greater importance: the problem of poverty and the solutions he imagined. The great sin of the lover, Shaw declared, was loving one person, rather than everyone. Shaw was determined to spread his love, however thinly, to all humanity by means of his socialism.

After many flirtatious relationships, Shaw had decided on a celibate life when he met, at age forty, Charlotte Payne-Townshend, a fellow Fabian and Anglo-Irish heiress. Their mutual socialist friends Sydney and Beatrice Webb introduced Shaw to Miss Payne-Townshend, who was an ardent supporter of women's rights. Shaw was initially reluctant, but she pursued him, and he eventually agreed to marry her, in 1898: She was the one who proposed and even supplied the ring. The marriage was never consummated, something that both apparently wanted. She did not want children and wanted to avoid any possibility of conceiving. The marriage was unorthodox but happy, with Payne-Townshend performing both secretarial and nursing roles for Shaw, who was frequently ill. They lived together in Ayot St. Lawrence, a small village in Hertfordshire, until her death in 1943.

THE INFLUENCE OF IBSEN

Victorian drama was profoundly affected by the introduction of Ibsen, the Norwegian playwright, onto the London stage in 1889. Shaw recognized and was deeply moved by the theatrical revolution Ibsen stirred up. The performance of *A Doll House* in London that year inspired Harley Granville-Barker, an actor and playwright friend of Shaw's, to recall it as "the most important dramatic event of the decade," as Peter Raby notes. The impact of Ibsen caused a huge separation in the dramatic community, dividing playwrights, actors, managers, and critics. On the one hand, Ibsen was praised for the social modernity and piercing individualism that he bestowed upon his characters. On the other hand, the images he conjured, such as a mother deserting her children in *A Doll House*, made others less enthusiastic about his form of modernity.

Clearly Shaw's philosophy and theater were greatly influenced by Ibsen. Ibsen's tragedies about middle-class individuals vibrated with tense relationships and earnest characters. Shaw found Ibsen's nonconformity, so vividly expressed in his drama, attractive and compatible with his own thinking. Shaw loathed the unquestioning acceptance of conventional morality. Ibsen's idea that humanity often loses touch with religiously grounded guidelines for behavior and moves to rigid rules of conduct, which conflict with the original lost ideals, resonated with Shaw. In *The Quintessence of Ibsenism*, published in 1891, Shaw evaluates Ibsen's dramatic aims and methods. He sees the world that Ibsen has created onstage — the world that Shaw himself would create — as "the empire of Man asserting the eternal validity of his own will." Shaw's heroic realist is a man of action whose strength of will commands the circumstances and individuals around him, directing them forward to a better future.

TURN TO THE THEATER

The artist and world-class playwright George Bernard Shaw emerged from the philosopher who was influenced by Ibsen, the journalist who reviewed music and plays, and the socialist who tried to solve the world's problems in his preliminary experiments with theater. Specifically, Shaw wanted to create worlds onstage in which Ibsen's philosophy could be enlivened and applied. Shaw's fascination with the theater developed in London. In fact he acted in some plays staged by the literary and socialist societies to which he subscribed. He writes, as Holroyd notes, that the stage is where "existence touches you delicately to the very heart, and where mysteriously thrilling people, secretly known to you in dreams of your childhood, enact a life in which terrors are as fascinating as delights; so that ghosts and death, agony and sin, become like love and victory, phases of an unaccountable victory." The stage appealed to Shaw. It was a world dominated by words: words responsible for creating worlds and people and changing both in a phrase and a line. In fact, Shaw's preferred theatrical form was the melodrama, where the key actions of the play all occur offstage so that the plot is driven entirely by dialogue and witty repartee. When a pivotal moment in the action occurred, it was often announced by telegram, or by other key players.

Shaw was less concerned with action than with what motivated a human being to action. To get a handle on motivations, he took a page out of Ibsen's book. Ibsen followed the structure of a conventional play, but in the third act of the play, where reconciliation is expected, Ibsen produced dialogue. So, for instance, Nora in *A Doll House* says, "We must sit down and discuss all this that has been happening between us." Instead of reconciling herself to the domesticity of the household, she marks out her individualism.

Shaw, too, had actions produce words — dialogue — as opposed to actions producing merely more actions, which was the habit of the conventional theater. Like Ibsen, Shaw's desire to change the world was preceded by his will to change the theater. William Archer, a theater critic of the time, believed that the future of drama lay in realism. Shaw sought to replace the conventional London play, which was full of romantic sentimentalism or meaningless humor, with his own brand of realism. According to Holroyd, when Sydney Oliver learned that Shaw was writing plays, he commented to a friend, "I was surprised because the quality of British playwriting, and the deadly artificiality and narrow convention of native contemporary British drama were at the time so repellant to me that I could not imagine any man with the intelligence of Shaw . . . conceiving that there was any possibility . . . for expressing himself in that medium."

Yet the influence of Ibsen and his theatrical revolution on the Norwegian stage prompted the optimist in Shaw to attempt a similar revolution. For his part, Shaw wanted to create art that explained how the shackles of society not only confined but also weighed down human beings. Holroyd quotes Shaw: "Art should refine our sense of character and conduct, of justice, and sympathy [while it heightens] our self-knowledge, self-control, precision of action, and considerateness [making us] intolerant of baseness, cruelty, injustice, and intellectual superficiality or vulgarity . . . by supplying works of a higher beauty and a higher interest than have yet been perceived [the artist] succeeds after a brief struggle with its strangeness, in adding this fresh extension of sense to the heritage of the race." Doing this was Shaw's attempt at a revolution in the arts, specifically the dramatic arts.

CONVENTIONAL BRITISH DRAMA AND SHAW

Shaw's dramatic revolution had many points of attack. He was against the conventional mechanics of Victorian drama, against the society that it depicted, against the morality that defined that society, and against the individuals who uncritically accepted the whole kit and caboodle. Shaw used the stage to make his case for a new system of social morality. To Shaw, art for art's sake is useless. Rather, art should derive from real life so that real people can learn from it and alter the world in which they live. It was this viewpoint that prompted Shaw to claim that journalism was the highest form of literary art. It was exquisitely anchored in the here and now.

"I created nothing; I invented nothing . . . I simply discovered drama in real life," Shaw explained, as Holroyd notes. Shaw's realism extended to institutions, society, and social ills with his concern with slums, prostitution, and the middle class. Yet when it ventured into the affairs of actual human beings, Shaw neglects to account for human nature. His realism, therefore, often becomes stylized and affected where human beings are concerned. To be fair, Shaw admitted that he intended his plays to be both didactic and allegorical. Thus, it may not have been Shaw's intention to represent the human struggle in his plays, but rather to represent the formation of an idea and its reception in conventional society. In Victorian society, immorality was merely a deviation from customs. So customs, which were expressed on the stage, needed to be reevaluated.

Countering the Well-Made Play

Right of Shaw's left-centered plays stood conventional Victorian drama. These so-called well-made plays were either romantic comedies culminating in marriage or sentimental and tragic dramas in which a fallen woman or man is ejected from society by a socially respectable figure, typically a titled gentleman. The plays followed a predictable formula: First, the key players of a play are introduced, often by minor figures like servants or chambermaids discussing the affairs of their masters. Then a dramatic situation arises in which characters misunderstand a very crucial part of the dramatic action. Then follows an exposition in which the misunderstanding is taken to its logical ends. A concluding scene reconciles the different viewpoints to produce a harmonious resolution. Well-made plays were very fashionable in London's West End.

Shaw not only deviated from the structure of these plays, he also denounced the suppositions on which they were based as false and replaced them with his own point of view. In contrast, Oscar Wilde, his fellow Irishmen, who was equally displeased with the phoniness of Victorian morality, took the absurdities of Victorian society on its own terms. He created a well-made play and through the use of language, epigrams, and comedy poked holes through high society's "truths." Wilde filled his conventionally constructed plays with an unconventional ethic. Though he maintained the traditional form of a well-made play, the essence of Wilde's plays revealed a morality grounded in charity and redemption of the heart and psyche.

Shaw insisted that his plays were not well-made plays because they focused on conflict and the *natural* development of that conflict.

Shaw criticized conventional plays for following a formulaic plot without allowance for human complexity: They always begin at the same point and always end at the same point. The only variable in their structure was the choice of language. They were crudely oversimplified and mechanical; what they depicted was not real life. "In such cheap wares I do not deal," he scornfully wrote in the preface to *Plays Pleasant and Unpleasant*.

To counter the well-made play that began with exposition, Shaw dove headlong into the action of the story, beginning in the middle of the story. Such an exciting start immediately draws in the audience. Then a causal chain of confusions, complications, or surprises follows, astonishing the characters as well as the audience and drawing the play to its end. Shaw believed that action drives the play to its conclusion, almost like a mathematical proof whose conclusion is inevitable and built into the steps that precede it. This impetus, which Shaw explained as biological and indeed evolutionary, is referred to as "the Life Force."

Theater of Ideas

In content, Shaw's chief criticism of conventional drama was that it put artificiality where reality should be, causing audiences to accept artifice as reality. In accepting artifice, audiences neglected truth. Yet an unpleasant truth is what Shaw sought to reveal onstage. Shaw's realism has often been termed social and psychological realism. That is, Shaw's heroes are discrete individuals defined by their psychology and their society. Thus, when they react to a given society, they do so in a way that coincides with their own true nature, not by subscribing to conventional moral formulas. Rather, they exert their will over society because their will can dominate that society.

Of course, Shaw also created characters that represented the follies of the society that he was criticizing. Such characters do not exert their will as the hero does; consequently they appear weak. By juxtaposing players and ideas in a new way, Shaw meant for his plays to lead to the progression of ideas in society. In conventional drama, the moral was the same every time, with a victory for society either in the form of marriage or the exile of a scarlet woman, thus protecting the society she infected. Unlike conventional dramatists, the feminist in Shaw often made the women of his plays the strongest characters. In his preface to *Man and Superman*, Shaw wrote that Ann, the play's heroine, was every woman and the true heart of the play. In his plays, women are enlivened with mystery, with images and dreams.

The influence of Wagner's *The Ring of the Nibelungs* can be seen in Shaw's plays. Shaw divided Wagner's characters into four types, which Shaw himself allegorizes as characters of his own plays. First, there are the dwarfs, who are greedy, predatory, instinctive, and dominated by passion; then there are giants, those mechanically toiling and stupid creatures who march along the road to life without thought, accepting everything as par for the course; third, there are the gods, who invent the codes of morality, justice, and law that Shaw seeks to dismantle. Finally, there is the free and independent hero, who by strength of will and intellect transcends the arbitrary codes created by the third class of people, wins over the second class of people, and orders and checks the first class of people. In this skeletal form, all four classes of people are found in Shaw's drama.

In setting characters and ideas against one another, Shaw was merely living up to his profession as a playwright: to bring meaning and order to events and situations. Shaw writes in the preface to his play *The Six of Calais* that the purpose and structure of a play varies depending on the aim of the playwright: "The highbrowed dramatic poet wants to make [life] intelligible and sublime. The farce writer wants to make it funny. The melodrama merchant wants to make it as exciting as some people find the police news. The pornographer wants to make it salacious." Each of these elements expresses itself in Shaw's drama.

SHAVIAN PHILOSOPHY

Shaw's childhood, the era in which he lived, his early interest in Marx and later Nietzsche, and even his wit and charm all mingled to form Shaw's philosophy, a philosophy that merits its own adjective: *Shavian.* Though Shavian philosophy does have a metaphysical aspect, it is primarily about style. As Holroyd quotes Shaw, the Shavian man "is magnificently endowed with the superb quality which we dishonor by the ignoble name of Cheek — a quality which has enabled men from time immemorial to fly without wings, and to live sumptuously without incomes."

Shaw's philosophy often involved snatching the most sublime moments of the human experience from the heights of heaven and drawing them down to earth — flying without wings so to speak — with the thought that heaven could be re-created on earth. Humanity momentarily soars to invincibility, or something close to perfection, in the form of love, power, or glory, only to tumble to earth. The dream, it seems, does not last, though Shaw set out to prove it was not a dream but rather an impending reality — a potential that could be realized with the proper strength of will. Shaw thought that nothing, not even heaven, was unknown to man. So he, as a playwright, was going to find out exactly what heaven was and, like Prometheus, bring it down to earth, to man. In one of his plays, in fact, he steals heaven and hell to re-create it onstage.

This division of the ideals of heaven and the realities of earth often emerges in his plays. Shaw fought to reconcile these two opposing philosophies. On the same day, Shaw was observed reading Marx's *Das Kapital* while learning the orchestral score to Wagner's *Tristan and Isolde* — a striking example of this Shavian conjunction. He took Wagner out of his mystic heights of love and lows of tragedy and threw him into the pragmatic, economic world of Karl Marx. On the one hand, Shaw was willing to abandon individualism for socialism, and on the other, he remarked in *The Quintessence of Ibsenism* that "the way to Communism lies through the most resolute and uncompromising Individualism."

Shavian Etiquette

In terms of conduct, Shavian etiquette means always being polite, which is a mark of superiority over unpleasant people; not wasting time with that which is boring or dull; not bothering with religion; and above all, self-sufficiency to the very end. Further, it is crucial to be cool and detached from every situation so that you may judge it objectively as an outsider. This means that you are not pained if the situation fails to resolve itself favorably. Shavian etiquette, common to Shaw's heroes and heroines, can be seen as a reaction against his dreary youth. He needed nobody's careful thought and gave few his own consideration. In creating a divide between his inner self, which he hid from the world, and his Shavian self, which he presented to society, his life became one great performance, one great affectation. Paradoxically, this was his precise criticism of aristocratic London society: its pretense. Shaw put on a giant pose and unpretentious airs — though airs nonetheless — for nearly everybody he knew. He would present himself with humor and insincerity, so it was difficult for people to understand or know exactly what or who he was. Given this, Oscar Wilde's famous epigram about Shaw shines with insight, "Bernard Shaw is an excellent man; he has not an enemy in the world, and none of his friends like him."

Regardless, Shaw was known for his wit and charm. If he had no truly close friends, he did have an entourage of fans, actors, journalists, and women to keep his solitude at bay. Shaw's irony and humor often drew people to him. Yet he became so renowned for his comedy that he feared London society would no longer take his plays seriously. He did want to elicit laughter, but an uncomfortable laughter. This Shavian quality is essential to his drama. For almost anytime a joke is being told, the audience or reader should cut through the laughter to find a truth, a tragic truth perhaps. In this way, Shaw placed grief under the heading of humor, as he would with all his most profound opinions of the world. "Almost all my greatest ideas have occurred to me first as jokes," he wrote in *Unpublished Shaw*.

IDEALS AND REALITY

A common theme in Shaw's plays is the tension created when the airiness of illusions and dreams are measured against the cold hard ground of reality. This tension is seen in Shaw's own life. He often evaded the facts of his life, blocking out the truth so that he would not have to endure its emotional hardship. For instance, when his mother and her adulterous lover, her voice instructor Vandeleur Lee, left to live together at one point, Shaw did not admit that his mother was having an extramarital affair. Instead, he made up an unlikely financial explanation.

On the other hand, when it came to matters that he willingly made public — like the content of his plays or his Fabianism, he was a determined realist. The contradiction between his realism and his idealism can be seen in a passion play he began writing, but never completed. In the play, written in blank verse, Judas and Jesus are engaged in conversation. Each character represents two opposing forces within the playwright himself, which he sought to reconcile. On the one hand, Judas is a destructive self-deluded man who is corrupted by the world around him. On the other, Christ is drawn forward in the direction of hope by some unknown future and unknown cause — unknown in Shaw's worldview at least, which did not admit the existence of God. Shaw paints Christ as a man of imagination through whom we attain reality. In other words, ideals — such as imagination and hope — do have a basis in reality. And they can somehow create realism out of their idealism. The mystery by which this is done is what fascinated Shaw. Uniting these oppositions was at once an obstacle and an inspiration for the genesis of Shaw's plays. At times, in his plays, seemingly irreconcilable ideas slide into one another. At other times, they are smashed into each other, and the audience watches the destruction that ensues when the world of ideals slips into the reality of things.

PLAYS UNPLEASANT

In his preface to *Mrs. Warren's Profession*, Shaw denounced poverty as the crime against man and society, with social order as the chief perpetrator. This theme carries the day in *Mrs. Warren's Profession* (1893). It is one of three plays in Shaw's first set of published theatrical works, entitled *Plays Unpleasant*. These plays explore the lowly lives of criminals, or those who are otherwise outcasts, and they provide valuable insights into the mind of Shaw the neophyte socialist.

In Victorian London, prostitution received a great deal of press coverage, and the brothel was an established institution. Indeed, in his preface to the play, Shaw insisted that the morality of his play would hold even if Mrs. Warren's profession were something less seedy. Shaw likens prostitution to "bookkeeping" — and he discusses the immorality of both for their indifference to their ideological consequences. Shaw meant to expose the hypocrisy of a system of social morality that was based on the ownership of land. Such a system, he believed, rather curiously, even caused the social evil of prostitution.

MRS. WARREN'S PROFESSION

In *Mrs. Warren's Profession*, Shaw saw prostitution as the net effect of that great economic evil: capitalism. Somebody loses the capitalism game, and in this case, it is Mrs. Warren, who, however, is not the victimized and frail figure that the reader would expect her to be. Rather, she is bold and commanding, successful and independent. She has raised a daughter, Vivie, who, despite not knowing the identity of her father, rose through society to receive various honors from Cambridge University.

Not only is Vivie ignorant of her father's identity, she is unaware of the nature of her mother's profession. Shaw created a rather prim and puritanical lady in young Vivie Warren, whom her mother calls a "stuck-up prude." Shaw was building the drama that would tumble into crisis when the inevitable revelation of Mrs. Warren's profession occurs. When Vivie takes the first step toward earning her own independence and self-respect, it results in a quarrel with her mother in which Mrs. Warren demands, "Do you know who you're speaking to, Miss." This question gives Vivie the opportunity to slash back with, "No. Who are you? What are you?" The revelation of Mrs. Warren's profession follows, and surprisingly, Vivie is touched by her mother's story. For Shaw, the story provides the rational basis for which impoverished women turn to prostitution: Mrs. Warren explains that her options were working "in a lead factory twelve hours a day for nine shilling a week until [I] die of lead poisoning," or earning a prostitute's income where she could wear "long fur coats, elegant and comfortable, with a lot of sovereigns in [my] purse." The choice does not seem like a choice at all. Of course, the turn to prostitution would not only be justified, but would be justified by anyone with a social conscience! And Shaw does seem to dismiss from the play the common critique that prostitution itself is immoral. As Vivie assures her mother, "[Y]ou were certainly quite justified — from the business point of view."

Vivie is touched by her mother's struggle and her victory against poverty because it has resulted in the charmed life that she has lived as a result. "My dear mother: you are a wonderful woman — you are stronger than all England," she states after her mother's revelation. But Vivie soon finds the mother she has just justified repulsive. Through a conversation with Sir George Crofts, the closest thing to a villain that Shaw ever wrote, it becomes clear to Vivie that her mother and Crofts are running brothels across Europe. They are profiting from the exploitation of young courtesan girls. Vivie is in disbelief. Though it was morally justifiable for her mother to act as she did to establish her place in society, what her mother is doing now with young girls is horrible. She is denying girls that were like her the same independence and self-respect that she now enjoys — and she is doing this to turn a tidy profit. Unable to face this contradiction, Vivie flees to her business offices in London.

In a symbolic gesture that condemns capitalism, Vivie rejects her monthly allowance from her mother, now that she knows it is money her mother has gotten from exploiting poor young girls. In deciding to pursue a life of virtuous independence, she must cast aside her past and begin life anew.

Rising above rather than yielding to a flawed society is a theme to which Shaw perpetually returns in drawing the line between his heroes or heroines and plodders. As Shaw wrote in the preface to *Mrs. Warren's Profession*, "It is true that in *Mrs. Warren's Profession*, Society, and not any individual, is the villain of the piece; but it does not follow that the people who take offence at it are all champions of society." To Shaw, society always seems to be the villain, and those who are bested by it are the weak-minded and inconsequential. Those who best it are the strong and engaged heroes that humans should, one and all, strive to be.

ARMS AND THE MAN: THE FOLLY OF IDEALS

Arms and the Man (1894) is one of Shaw's three *Pleasant Plays*, which explore the lives of those who are tragicomically delusional, who aspire to false ideals and have those ideals burst before them. The influence of Ibsen is evident in these plays as Shaw shows codes of conduct out of sync with human experience and how following such false standards results in unnatural and affected behavior. To counter this pretense, Shaw offers his own approach in which pragmatism and instinct are seen as above fantasy and ideals.

The two main characters (and the embodiment of the ideals in this play) are Raina and Sergius, members of Bulgarian high society, who are engaged to be married. Raina is a sentimental young woman who has deluded herself with the romance of war and love. When she learns that her beau led the charge against the Serbian enemy combatants, she exclaims, "I am so happy! So proud! It proves that all our ideas were real after all . . . patriotism. Our heroic ideals." Understanding the division between the world of ideas and the world of reality will be Raina's moral lesson by the play's end.

Sergius is equally sentimental: He follows a code of chivalrous conduct appropriate for the nineteenth-century gentry. The gentle and adoring Raina appears to love Sergius, and Sergius is equal in his adoration of Raina. But as the play progresses, the way in which they express their love for each other contrasts with what they do when each thinks the other isn't looking, calling into question the sincerity of their love. Sergius, for instance, flirts shamelessly with Louka, the servant girl. Sergius and Raina set each other up as the king and queen, respectively, in a world of their creation. "My hero! My king," gushes Raina, to which Sergius responds, "My queen!" Unfortunately, the real world does not align with their fantasy. The tension mounts as the viewer is left to wonder whether the hero and heroine are also skeptical of each other's loyalty and sincerity. Will each of them be exposed for the poseurs that they are? And what happens then, when they are forced to live in the real world?

Sergius has just returned from the battlefield, where he led the main charge against the hostile Serbians, resulting in a victory for the Bulgarians. Yet, once it becomes clear that his cavalry charge was more suicidal than brave, darker layers of his persona are revealed. When he runs the risk of not having his rank elevated, he falls into a gloomy mood. In the next scene, he shamelessly flirts with Louka, the beautiful servant girl, despite his professions of love for Raina. Louka, a cynic and a realist, warns Sergius, "I don't want your kisses. Gentlefolk are all alike: you making love to me behind Miss Raina's back; and she doing the same behind yours." This revelation shocks Sergius, as it does the audience. Despite his own questionable behavior, he cannot shake the pose that he has struck, and he responds, "Please remember that a gentleman does not discuss the conduct of the lady he is engaged to with her maid." The formality of his lines contrasts vividly with his willingness to compromise himself. Louka chides him once more, and the truth that the audience has been squinting to see becomes clear. "I know the differences between the sort of manner you and she put on before one another and the real manner," she tells him.

Bluntschli, the Unsentimental Realist

Set against the calculating idealism of Sergius is the unsentimental realism of Bluntschli, a Serbian soldier. Bluntschli first enters the play as a terrified fugitive. Raina is sitting at her windowsill, giddy as she watches the battle. At this point, Bluntschli bursts into her room from outside, seeking refuge. In contrast to Sergius' apparent bravado, Bluntschli appears a coward. Yet as the scene progresses, the viewer feels compassion for Bluntschli. His action seems more human, while Sergius' actions begin to seem like poses. When Bluntschli reveals to Raina that Sergius' cavalry run was nearly suicidal, Sergius' heroism dissolves into nihilism. Bluntschli's instinct is for life, while Sergius' is for death — and through this, the audience sees where realism on the one hand and idealism on the other meet their logical ends.

Bluntschli's sudden entrance disturbs Raina's imaginative fantasy, bursting the bubble of her idealism with his pragmatism. He is no patriot and does not fight for the glory or romance of war. He does not even carry ammunition with him, but rather stuffs his pockets with chocolate, which prompts Raina to give him the nickname "my chocolate cream soldier." He is not even a Serbian, but rather a Swiss mercenary plying his trade — a businessman of sorts. Bluntschli is the enemy, and it is Raina's patriotic duty to turn him over to the guards. But Bluntschli pleads for his life, and through her compassion, she spares him. She conspires for him to escape with her mother. The audience later learns that Raina has fallen in love with Bluntschli: She drops her picture in his coat pocket before he leaves — a coat he had stolen from Raina's father's closet.

When Bruntschli comes back to return the stolen coat, he accuses Raina of pretending and lying, as Louka did Sergius earlier, and the illusory nature of Raina's love for Sergius is revealed. Raina wonders how Bruntschli has found her out. "Instinct, dear young lady," he tells her. "Instinct, and experience of the world." Pragmatism and instinct are the essence of Shaw's hero in this play.

Given that Raina creates role after role for herself, it is difficult to pierce through her pretense to the core of her character. Shaw himself put the case best when he wrote in an essay, "A Dramatic Realist to his Critics," published in Eric Bentley's *Bernard Shaw*, that "In the play of mine which is most in evidence in London just now, the heroine has been classified by critics as a minx, a liar, and a poseur. I have nothing to do with that: the only moral question for me is, does she do good or harm? If you admit that she does good, that she generously saves a man's life and wisely extricates herself from a false position with another man, then you may classify her as you please." In choosing to marry Bluntschli over Sergius, Raina chooses reality over artifice. This is a long way from the sentiment contained in her words at the onset of the play. Once she realizes what an imposter Sergius is, she embraces the real world and its Shavian embodiment in Bluntschli. The play's last words are Sergius', the play's antihero, who remarks with wonder about Bluntschli, "What a man! Is he a man?" The idea of what constitutes a man reoccurs in Shaw's work.

By commanding his environment, exhibiting honor, courage, and a cool realism driven by instinct, Bluntschli is wholly Shavian and wholly human. Through him, therefore, the audience hears the ring of truth.

PLAYS FOR PURITANS: THE DEVIL'S DISCIPLE

Shaw's chief criticism of Victorian drama was that it assumed an arbitrary social morality. *The Devil's Disciple* (1897) is the first of Shaw's *Plays for Puritans*. In these plays, Shaw created heroes who transcended and replaced the prevailing moral creeds. The plays occur during times of war and explore the morality involved in justice, vengeance, and violence. Because these plays are melodramas, the central action of the plays are kept offstage and announced through telegrams or the declarations of other key players onstage. These plays culminate in a trial scene, where the conventional morality of the society collapses and is replaced with Shaw's morality — essentially the ethics of the New Testament, minus God.

The Devil's Disciple is set in a small puritan community of New Hampshire during the American Revolution in October 1777. In the first act, Mrs. Dudgeon is introduced, and the news of her husband's death is received with the dourness of her own dead Puritanism. Her son, Christy, breaks the news to her. He is met with this response: "Well, I do think this is hard on me — very hard on me. His brother, that was a disgrace to us all his life, gets hanged on the public gallows as a rebel; and your father, instead of staying at home where his duty was, with his own family, goes after him and dies, leaving everything on my shoulders. After sending this girl to me to take care of, too! It's sinful, so it is; downright sinful." The little girl, Essie, was her brother-in-law's (the hanged rebel) illegitimate child, whom Mrs. Dudgeon must now care for. To make Mrs. Dudgeon's plight all the worse, her second detested son, for whom the play was named, has been left his father's property and wealth. This second son, Richard "Dick" Dudgeon, is deaf to Mrs. Dudgeon's moral tyranny. He represents a system so at odds with her own formal Puritanism that she is driven to say that her son will, essentially, burn in hell. He, in turn, cuts through her hypocrisy with, "Well, Mother: keeping up appearances as usual? That's right, that's right."

Mrs. Dudgeon is a woman of strict principles. Her son, Dick, is her opposite in this regard, as he acts according to instinct. He represents the counter to her overwrought idealism. In the climax of the play, Dick follows his instinct to the point of death and yet prevails as a saint.

The play takes place during the American Revolutionary War, and the British army has occupied the little New Hampshire town. They are weeding out the rebels and hanging them. It is rumored that the British are more concerned with making an example of someone than with seeking those who are actually disloyal to King George, and that Dick, a known sinner, may soon be among the executed. Anthony Anderson, the town minister, meets with Dick to warn him. During the course of their meeting, the minister leaves for town, and Dick is left alone with Judith Anderson, the minister's wife. Judith despises Dick for reasons similar to Mrs. Dudgeon's, so this is very unpleasant for her. Dick notes wryly that an unsuspecting passerby would mistake them for husband and wife. Sure enough, someone does. Suddenly, British militiamen pound on the door with a warrant for the minister's arrest. And in a Dickensian twist, Dick gives himself up as Minister Anderson. Furthermore, he forces Judith to remain silent about the mistaken identification, so that the minister will never find out that Dick saved his life.

Torn and unable to justify Dick's sacrifice, Judith tells her husband, who instantly sets off to some mysterious destination. Rather than fleeing like a coward, as Judith disgustedly assumed he did, Anderson returns and orders the sergeant to "stop the execution. I am Anthony Anderson, the man you want." Later in this scene, the audience learns that Anderson was responsible for a rebel raid against the British in a neighboring town, which resulted in a British defeat and an edict of safe conduct for Anderson. The militiamen cannot execute him.

Once the trial is resolved, and both Anderson and Dick are released from custody, Dick returns Anderson's coat to him, the coat that he took from Anderson's house when he was falsely arrested. Anderson, however, says to him, "Your mother told me, Richard, that I should never have chosen Judith if I'd been born for the ministry. I am afraid she was right: so, by your leave, you may keep my coat and I'll keep yours." He chooses a life *without* the ministry. The coat swap is a symbolic identity swap.

Richard has become a minister of sorts. He is a saint who embodies the ideals of self-sacrifice and near martyrdom. He leads humanity to greater heights. In a more local sense, Anderson has done a similar deed for the rebels. He emerges as the hero whose efforts have led to the rebels' victory against the British.

In typical melodramas, characters conform to stereotypical roles meant to elicit rote reactions from the audience. There is the character who audiences are meant to hate, the one they are meant to pity, and finally, the one they are meant to admire. In Shaw's drama, however, the roles are less clear. Dick is a hero in Shaw's sense, and the minister is a hero in a military sense. But could Judith be a heroine? And who is meant to be hated and who pitied? By leaving theatergoers with these questions, Shaw imposed moral responsibility on them, which was uncomfortable and unexpected for Victorian audiences.

The Devil's Disciple was first produced in New York City, and it was a huge success. Indeed, it was Shaw's first financial success as a playwright. In this play, as in his other two *Plays for Puritans*, Shaw presented characters who, by virtue of their strength of will, commanded the worlds of those around them, improved those worlds, and, in so doing, were elevated to the rank of heroes. This was the message with which Shaw intended to enlighten his audience. Daniel Dervin, in *Shaw: A Psychological Study*, quotes the playwright: "The whole character of the piece must be allegorical, idealistic, full of generalizations and moral lessons: and it must represent conduct as producing swiftly and certainly on the individual the results which in actual life it only produces on the race in the course of many centuries." In his play, Shaw crystallizes this process with his ending — that *The Devil's Disciple* ends in Britain's defeat is Shaw's sly signal that the clutches of British society will be released through heroic individualism.

MAN AND SUPERMAN: PLAY AS POLITICAL TREATISE

Shaw defied every convention of Victorian theater when he wrote *Man and Superman* (1902–03), which embodies the quintessence of his philosophy. In this drama, Shaw perfected the medium in which he best expressed himself. This play is a dialogue in which ideas are tossed back and forth, with an undercurrent of drama that is weak compared to the strong ideas from which the drama arises. According to Shaw's friend Beatrice Webb, as Holroyd quotes her, in *Man and Superman*, Shaw "has found his form: a play which is not a play; but only a combination of essay, treatise, interlude, lyric — all these different forms illustrating one central idea."

Many of Shaw's plays have been interpreted in terms of his social and political philosophies. *Mrs. Warren's Profession*, for instance, is a social critique of capitalism. *The Devil's Disciple* criticizes social morality. In the development of such political philosophy, the answers to the questions that arise in *Man and Superman* must be answered before the larger questions posed by his other plays are tended to.

The Life Force versus Fantasy

Man and Superman begins with rather conventional themes, with questions of courtship, a secret marriage, and a token romantic artist with an antiquated name. The play is famous, however, for the dream sequence of the third act: Don Juan, a parallel to Jack Tanner, the Shavian hero of the main part of the play, is set against the Devil, Tanner's antithesis in many ways. Like Tanner, Don Juan is a social outcast, which the Devil alludes to when he says, "Curious how these clever men, whom you would have supposed born to be popular here, have turned out social failures like Don Juan." On the one hand, the Devil implies that Don Juan is a social outcast. On the other, the Devil is challenging Don Juan's entire project, predicting that his desire to reform society will end in abject failure. A debate ensues among them where the Devil emerges as a lover of fantasy and pleasure, and Don Juan advocates the evolution of a higher form of the species through the Life Force.

The "Life Force" is a Shavian doctrine in which true heroes must consult their consciences, morals, and intellects and drive the course of progress with their will to power. According to Don Juan, in order to divert the course of human progress to its proper ends, it is necessary for humanity to undergo a moral revolution. Conventional morality has clearly failed if it has produced the pretensions belonging to Victorian society. What society has dubbed as the pursuit of happiness has led to misery. Thus it is an illusion, a pale reflection, of where the road to happiness truly lies. As Tanner says earlier in the first act of the play, anticipating Don Juan's criticism, "But a lifetime of happiness! No man alive could bear it: it would be hell on earth."

It is through the intellect that a new of notion of happiness is forged, accurately based on reality. Forging reality by destroying illusions is Don Juan's primary game. As he says, "Nothing is real here. That is the horror of damnation." Don Juan uses individuals as a means to the end of a better world. He proposes to alter the essence of humanity.

Reason versus Emotion

Contrary to Don Juan, the Devil treats people as ends in themselves, not as means. In his system, where things in themselves are valued, Don Juan's plan to alter human nature seems dangerous, if not impossible. The Devil believes achieving this change could destroy human nature itself. "And is man any the less destroying himself for all this boasted brains of his?" the Devil challenges Don Juan. The Devil implies that by making a god out of reason, man corrupts his nature, a nature that cannot be explained away in purely rational terms. That sort of system ends in death and decay: "There is nothing in Man's industrial machinery but his greed and sloth; his heart is in his weapons. This marvelous force of Life of which you boast is a force of Death." Alongside reason and intellect, there must be a place for emotions, beauty, and love in the soul and conscience of man — yet, it is precisely these sentimentalities that Don Juan despises.

Though Shaw intended for Don Juan to win the debate, the Devil's parting words to Don Juan make the denouement ambiguous. Don Juan, who is leaving, prefers a life driven by the Life Force rather than one of plodding boredom, which he finds when he is constricted morally by heaven and hell. The Devil's farewell to Don Juan warns of "the punishment of the fool who pursues the better before he has secured the good." That is, Don Juan is an idealist. Strangely, Don Juan himself explains and criticizes hell for a similar folly: "Hell is the home of the unreal and the seekers of happiness . . . here you are not an animal at all: you are a ghost, an appearance, an illusion, a convention, deathless, ageless . . . There are no social questions here, no political questions, no religious questions." The hedonism of hell, which holds beauty and sensations as its gods, has no appeal to the seeker of the Life Force. Though both speakers present arguments that may be flawed, Shaw's overarching message is that ideals cannot prevail in a world governed by real facts if there is no agent strong enough to shape reality such that humanity will come into contact with these ideals. The Devil worries that reality cannot be altered, while Don Juan's optimism is sure that it can be. In the final act of the play, the two extremes reach an amicable reconciliation.

Ann as the Life Force

In the final act, Shaw's Don Juan Tanner is bested by the cheeky and flirtatious Ann, Shaw's ideal heroine. Ann dominates reality and uses her own designs to alter its course. She embodies the Life Force as her instinct propels her to marriage and procreation with Tanner. Tanner says, "Vitality in a woman is a blind fury of creation." That the instinct to procreate and perpetuate a species that progresses with each succeeding generation resides in a woman suggests that women should be the natural heroines of Shaw's play. Further, Ann can exert her will, even if the means by which she does so are dishonest, while Tanner cannot when it comes to the biggest question of all, marriage. When he says, "Ann: I will not marry you," Ann retorts that nobody asked him his opinion on the matter. His own fate, which is in the hands of Ann, is already determined: "I chose you!" she tells him, and indeed her choice dictates a reality that Tanner will submit to.

In his review of *Man and Superman*, critic and actor Max Beerbohm Tree called the play Shaw's masterpiece-to-date, and many enthusiasts place the play at the center of Shaw's body of work. It contains, in full force, all the elements that are sprinkled throughout the rest of his plays, from the Don Juan hero, to the importance of the will, to the idea of a Life Force, to a dialectic of ideas. All these elements come together so that if Shaw is a successful playwright, the audience will reevaluate the moral dictums to which they abide. And they will question the legitimacy of the society that condones those dictums.

PYGMALION: THE HOPE OF SCIENCE

Shaw wrote *Pygmalion* (1912–13) at a climactic moment in his life. The plays he wrote in this era are among his best. Romantically, he was fiercely in love with the actress Mrs. Patrick Campbell. As Holroyd notes in his biography of Shaw, this was a fiery and passionate love as can be seen in Mrs. Campbell's response to Shaw's request that she play the lead role: "[Thank you for] thinking I can be your pretty slut." With the death of his mother, Shaw seemed to find an emotional replacement in Mrs. Campbell. Sadly, she would break his heart too, and, like his mother, instead of filling his heart, she emptied it of its contents. Historically, the curtain was about to fall on the relatively tranquil Edwardian era as the world was ratcheting itself up for World War I, a war that acted out the faulty romanticism, industrialism, and nationalism of the era that preceded it. This was the prelude to *Pygmalion*'s creation.

In his preface to the play, Shaw places a great deal of emphasis on phonetics, the "science of speech." As he writes in the preface to the play, "The reformer England needs today is an energetic phonetic enthusiast: that is why I have made such a one the hero of a popular play." This is a rather striking claim. Shaw was always very impressed by the influence of science, especially in the twentieth century. The power of science to change the world is one of the themes of *Pygmalion*. Shaw demonstrates how one specific science, phonetics, can undermine the entire British aristocracy.

Transformed by Science

Professor Henry Higgins plucks a cockney flower girl from the streets of London and nurtures her so she speaks like a duchess — science poses a threat to the old order by undermining it and proposing the possibility of a new order. Higgins and his friend, Colonel Pickering, place a bet to see if they can turn Eliza into a duchess, and then pass her off as one during a garden party held at Buckingham Palace. After months of work, they are successful in their cynical endeavor. The ideals of science come alive in Eliza as readers see the transformative power of phonetics make an independent woman out of an impoverished one. This change in class affects a moral change in Eliza, too, which is a recurrent theme in Shaw's plays: One must have money before one can truly be free to make a moral choice. In affording proper behavior, Shaw says that the premise of his play is "filling up the deepest gulf that separates class from class and soul from soul." Again, poverty is the problem that, this time, finds its solution in phonetics and science.

Eliza Doolittle is the heroine of Shaw's play. It is she who changes, and changes for the better, while the other characters remain unaffected by the great experiment that Higgins has conducted. Higgins himself does not change in this transformative experience. He has not learned what life should have taught him. He is not less condescending, nor more compassionate — his faults are in no way lessened.

Eliza Triumphant

At the beginning of the play, Higgins treats Eliza as little more than empirical data. When the kindhearted Colonel Pickering asks him "Does it occur to you, Higgins, that the girl has some feelings," Higgins responds, "Oh no, I don't think so." Eliza on the other hand becomes not only more poised and elegant but also her moral character actually improves. Her strident cockney accent in Act One is gone, and she has become a mature woman in Act Four, where the climax of the play occurs. The three — Eliza, Pickering, and Higgins — have just returned from the banquet, and the two men are discussing the great relief they now feel that the experiment is over. They refer to Eliza as if she were a seasonal centerpiece, some object to be stored away once done with, and not a human being at all. The men ramble on and on as Eliza stands back in the darkness, listening as they talk about her. They say things like, "I can go to bed at last without dreading tomorrow," and "no more artificial duchesses. The whole thing has been simple purgatory." Eliza, deeply hurt, violently lashes out against Higgins, and she falls to sobs of "What's to become of me," and "I've won your bet for you, haven't I? That's enough for you. *I* don't matter, I suppose." The exchange builds and reverses its social order until Eliza emerges in full command, with Higgins at her mercy saying, "It is you who have hit me. You have wounded me to the heart." Eliza feels triumphant and is at last the independent woman that Higgins wanted her to be, though for Higgins, the success is rather bittersweet because such independence means rising above Higgins himself.

Though she once depended on Higgins and his instruction to make her a better person, she has now bested him morally. She has transcended the gentlemen whose society she was aiming to enter. "I had only to lift my finger to be as good as you," she says to him. But surely she did more than that, which means that she is better than he. In response Higgins says, "By George, Eliza, I said I'd make a woman of you; and I have." In the beginning of the play, Eliza begs for money and her right to not starve, which Mr. Higgins coldly casts off: "A woman who utters such depressing and disgusting sounds has no right to be anywhere — no right to live . . . your native language is the language of Shakespeare and Milton and The Bible." Though she is denied the right to even live at the beginning of the play, by the play's end, she has grown into a lady who says, "Every girl has a right to be loved." The ideal of a master and disciple puts the pupil in a position of sanctity and reverence, an ideal that both Shaw and, by extension, Higgins held high. To corrupt that ideal with romance was too vulgar a thought for either man to bear, so Eliza does not marry Higgins.

Independent Woman

This is one explanation of the play's end, which was offered by Shaw himself. Another explanation places the emphasis on Eliza's moral superiority to Higgins. She is in the commanding position at the play's end, for Higgins now depends on her, while she no longer depends on him. His last words to her resonate with sadness because life has taught him nothing: "Oh, by the way, Eliza, order a ham and a Stilton cheese, will you? And buy me a pair of reindeer gloves, number eights, and a tie to match that new suit of mine, at Eale & Binman's. You can choose the color." She tells him to buy them himself and sweeps out. She will not choose the color because she does not choose a life of idle submission to Higgins. Higgins is breezily oblivious to the end, ignoring Eliza's refusal and assuredly telling his mother, "She'll buy 'em all right enough."

Shaw was so accustomed to his plays failing that when *Pygmalion* succeeded beyond expectations, he thought something must be wrong with it since everyone liked it. The one major difficulty with the play is that it has no ending, strictly speaking. Shaw had to return to it time and again, and he wrote a prose ending to add some sort of resolution to it. He has Eliza marry not Higgins but the kind, if absentminded, Freddy. It is strange that he was at a loss when it came to concluding the play, but his difficulties may have been complicated by his own recently wrecked romance with Mrs. Campbell. An optimistic ending in which Higgins marries "the pretty slut" would have been too heart-breaking to bear.

The production of the play was so difficult that at one point Shaw was on his knees demonstrating to Mrs. Campbell the motions she should use, and she cut back, as Holroyd notes, with "[T]hat's where I like to see my authors, on their knees at my feet!" So the play ends with a hollow chuckle. Higgins has lost the Eliza he once had, even if he is not willing to admit it outright. For the first time in Shaw's drama, words actually fail, and an empty laughter fills the void.

HEARTBREAK HOUSE: THE REACTION TO WORLD WAR I

Heartbreak House (1919), written during World War I, is Shaw's response to the war's devastation. In the play, characters find refuge from an unsympathetic reality in the world of their dreams, imaginations, and deceptions. Escaping from reality, of course, is merely a palliative, so the entire play has a sickly aura. For instance, in the first act of the play, Lady Utterword asks her brother-in-law what the dynamite she sees is for. He responds, "To blow up the human race if it goes too far." These eerie and ominous witticisms, scattered throughout the play, give a feeling of impending doom.

True to the title he gave it, Shaw describes *Heartbreak House* as a tragedy, similar to *King Lear*. Appropriately, there are three daughter figures — Ellie Dunn, Lady Utterword, and Mrs. Hushabye — and a father figure, Captain Shotover. Lady Utterword and Mrs. Hushabye are Captain Shotover's actual daughters, while Ellie Dunn is Mrs. Hushabye's friend. Ellie, modest both in fortune and bearing, has come to the house to speak to Mrs. Hushabye about Boss Mangan, a man whom she would like to marry. Mangan is a wealthy capitalist who has robbed Ellie's real father of his modest income, though both Ellie and her father are unaware of it. Ellie is so deceived that she is willing to marry Mangan in gratitude for him being "wonderfully good" to her father. Mangan himself tells her later, "I ruined him as a matter of business." Mrs. Hushabye describes Ellie as a "poor weak innocent" girl. Later, a dramatic change occurs in Ellie's character: She exerts her power over Mangan by forcing him to agree to marry her, and thereby changes the situation.

A Web of Deceit

Mrs. Hushabye refuses to give Ellie her blessing in marriage. She is bothered that Ellie is marrying the man for his wealth, not for his heart. Yet Mrs. Hushabye is not so soft and sentimental as this would make her appear. In fact, when Ellie first enters the house, she is greeted by Captain Shotover, who makes a telling remark about his daughter, Mrs. Hushabye, saying, "I keep this house, she upsets it." From the outset, then, Mrs. Hushabye is established as an agent of disorder, while her father, the captain, does his best to avoid destruction.

In a twist, when Mangan admits to Ellie that he ruined her father, he also admits that he is in love with the destructive siren Mrs. Hushabye, though she is revolted by him. Ellie plays on Mangan's attraction to Mrs. Hushabye by telling him that unless he marries Ellie he will never see Mrs. Hushabye again. Mrs. Hushabye would not see him otherwise but for the fact that he will soon be the husband of her good friend. Given that Mangan's decisions are made at the mercy of

Mrs. Hushabye's and Ellie's desires, he loses his autonomy of will. His heartbreak is the prelude to his death, as Ellie describes it: "His heart is breaking: that is all. It is a curious sensation: the sort of pain that goes mercifully beyond our powers of feeling. When your heart is broken, your boats are burned: nothing matters any more. It is the end of happiness and the beginning of peace."

Given their opposing natures and ideals, a quarrel inevitably occurs between Ellie and Mrs. Hushabye. In it, Mrs. Hushabye is exposed as a vapid woman who has "the trick of falling in with everyone's mood." In the presence of men, she is a siren; in the presence of Ellie, she acts maternally; in the presence of her equally dubious husband, Hector, she acts as a companion. She is molded by the circumstances and individuals that surround her. She is, at bottom, insincere and deceitful. Even her beautiful black hair is a deceit — a wig. Equally deceptive is her husband, Hector, who tells the imaginative Ellie lies about himself so that she falls in love with him. When Hector is revealed as a married fraud, worlds come crashing down for Ellie as her dream of love comes to ruin. But for Hector and Mrs. Hushabye, these games are commonplace, and waltzing into and out of reality affects them not at all.

Escape Through Dreams

Like Mrs. Hushabye and Hector, Captain Shotover is also tired of life, though because of his kind nature he expresses his exhaustion in less disastrous ways. In one of the more beautiful speeches in the play, he tells Ellie, "No: I dread being drunk more than anything in the world. To be drunk means to have dreams; to go soft; to be easily pleased and deceived; to fall into the clutches of women. Drink does that for you when you are young. But when you are old: very very old, like me, the dreams come by themselves. You don't know how terrible that is: you are young: you sleep at night only, and sleep soundly. But later on you will sleep in the afternoon. Later you will sleep even in the morning;

and you will awake tired, tired of life . . . you can awaken yourself with rum. I drink now to keep sober . . . Go get me another . . .You had better see for yourself the horror of an old man drinking." Ellie responds, "Dream. I like you to dream. You must never be in the real world when we talk together."

Here is the escape from the real world, a world that is paradoxically swimming in dreams. The heartbreaking characters are the ones who are caught in life's snares, unable to distill reality from dreams, dreams from reality.

The Voice of Realism

Set against Ellie's childishness and Mrs. Hushabye's and Hector's deception, is Lady Utterword's realism. Lady Utterword left Heartbreak House to marry her husband. In doing so, she renounced her family and the sickly ways in which the tenants of Heartbreak House operate. She immediately comes across as the voice of wisdom and the will when she says tells Ellie, "The important thing is not to have the last word, but to have your own way." That is, reality precedes principles, or at least should. The horror of *Heartbreak House* is that reality is hidden beneath lies, deceit, and dreams. Lady Utterword, entering it from the outside, brings reality and order to the house. She is its savior in this way. "I escaped young [from the house]," she says near the end of the play, "but it has drawn me back. It wants to break my heart too. But it shan't." Lady Utterword is not a victim of Heartbreak House, rather "she breaks hearts" as Hector says. She is coolly detached from the drama and sadness that surrounds the house.

She is like Shaw — or what he wanted to be — in her hardness and strength of character. She doesn't allow suffering to keep her from accepting only what she wills to affect her. When Ellie tells Captain Shotover, "I feel now as if there was nothing I could not do, because I want nothing," he responds, "That's the only real strength. That's genius. That's better than rum." Lady Utterword is able to do this. She is a woman of action who commands those around her. When Hector threatens to kill her because her command of reality is a threat to his desire to control life through lies, she responds, "I am not such a fool as I look." Nothing is as it seems. While Hector has to resort to a phony imagination to solve the problems of reality, Lady Underwood merely resorts to words and has what she wants at the tip of her tongue, "Well I can't smack Randall [her brother-in-law on her husband's side, whom she finds idle and useless]: he is too big; so when he gets nerves and is naughty, I just rag him till he cries. He will be all right now. Look: he is half asleep already." In the critical last scene, when a bomb is dropped that kills Mangan, each person's character is revealed for what it truly is: Hector and Mrs. Hushabye see the experience as all fun and games, saying "how damnably dull the world has become again suddenly" and "But what a glorious experience! I hope they'll come again tomorrow night." Captain Shotover muses philosophically and dreamily that "Courage will not save you; but it will shew that your souls are still alive." Lady Utterword brings her lapdog of a brother-in-law, Randall, back to reality with "The danger is over, Randall. Go to bed." Nothing, not even war, can puncture her matter-of-factness. Though she may come across as unfeeling, it is also a testament to her strength and courage — in short, her Shavian heroism.

Heartbreak House is much like a farce wherein deception and lies are taken as commonplace and normal. The harmony and order of this world are suggested only by their absence, and their absence begs for a return that is all but impossible. Previously, Shaw's plays hailed realism against idealism. Here realism, standing alone, becomes unbearable, so the characters reel away into their world of dreams. Though the play, which Shaw repeatedly referred to as his masterpiece, resonates with doom and destruction, a chord of optimism is struck in the last words of the play, spoken by Ellie: "Oh, I hope so." Against the menacing bombs, the destructive lies, the hearts breaking and realities quaking, Shaw offers the solace of hope.

CONCLUSION

Paradox lived in the heart and mind of George Bernard Shaw. Without his Shavian pose, Shaw admitted that he lacked its essence. Though the pain caused by these conflicts was surely great, as with any great playwright, it was the instinctive consciousness of just these inner conflicts that ultimately conspired to produce his greatest drama.

His first series of plays, *Plays Unpleasant*, addresses matters that were unspeakable in high society. To write about prostitution, adultery, and poverty was considered bad form. The Victorians receded into silence when a difficult moral question was placed before them. Shaw, on the other hand, staged the questions to have the audience explode into uncomfortable laughter. He left the audience struggling through such contradictions to find their own way out. However, in his own life, moral dilemmas were allowed to fade into the silence of neglect, even though he criticized such behavior in his society and onstage. In a letter he wrote to Ellen Terry, which Holroyd quotes, incest is implied when he writes, "If you were my mother, I am sure I should carry you away to the tribe in Central America where — but I have a lot of things to say . . ." This is yet another instance of the tension Shaw felt in reconciling the philosophical realism that he built up on the stage and the life he lived.

Though creating and controlling the lives and worlds that he exacted and enlivened on the stage, the events of Shaw's own life were often either out of his control or not, to him, worth controlling. In London, Shaw's drama was initially unsuccessful. One play after the other was denied production. Others began production only to be cut off since rehearsals were not progressing. If the plays made it to opening night, critics would chide Shaw for writing a philosophical essay in the form of a dialogue and passing that off as drama. Other critics went so far as to claim that Shaw was not a playwright. They said that his characters were lifeless, that staging a Shavian drama was impossible, and that the dramas he wrote could not be called plays. This was despite the fact that Shaw won the Nobel Prize for Literature in 1925 and an Oscar in 1939 for adapting *Pygmalion* to the big screen — the only person to win both awards.

Shaw fought against the accusation of intellectual narcissism by explaining that, like Ibsen, he created plays where words preceded action. Seldom did words produce action because of the conflict that existed in realizing the ideals that those words espoused. Silence, again, was one refuge. Yet, as Shaw explained, plays do not exist where there is no conflict. Shaw's most renowned plays examine "the tragic-comic irony of the conflict between real life and the romantic imagination," as Shaw writes in his preface to *Major Barbara* — with an eye to himself, perhaps.

In his old age, Shaw became a household name in Britain and Ireland and was renowned throughout the world. He spent his later years tending to the grounds of the house he had shared with his wife at Ayot St. Lawrence. At age ninety-four, Shaw fell from a tree while pruning it and injured himself. He died shortly thereafter from renal failure resulting from the fall. Shaw was cremated, and his ashes, mixed with those of his wife, were strewn along footpaths in their garden.

DRAMATIC MOMENTS

from the Major Plays

These short excerpts are from the playwright's major plays. They give a taste of the work of the playwright. Each has a short introduction in brackets that helps the reader understand the context of the excerpt. The excerpts, which are in chronological order, illustrate the main themes mentioned in the In an Hour essay.

from **Man and Superman** (1903)
Act Three

CHARACTERS

> The Devil
> Don Juan
> The Statue
> Ana

[In this play, Shaw takes on the Don Juan theme, personified by Jack Tanner, a bachelor who tries to resist the pursuit of Ann Whitefield. In this third act, which breaks the main action of the play and takes place in hell, Don Juan and the Devil appear and take up the major themes of the play.]

THE DEVIL: And is Man any the less destroying himself for all this boasted brain of his? Have you walked up and down upon the earth lately? I have; and I have examined Man's wonderful inventions. And I tell you that in the arts of life man invents nothing; but in the arts of death he outdoes Nature herself, and produces by chemistry and machinery all the slaughter of plague, pestilence and famine. The peasant I tempt today eats and drinks what was eaten and drunk by the peasants of ten thousand years ago; and the house he lives in has not altered as much in a thousand centuries as the fashion of a lady's bonnet in a score of weeks. But when he goes out to slay, he carries a marvel of mechanism that lets loose at the touch of his finger all the hidden molecular energies, and leaves the javelin, the arrow, the blowpipe of his fathers far behind. In the arts of peace Man is a bungler. I have seen his cotton factories and the like, with machinery that a greedy dog could have invented if it had wanted money instead of food. I know his clumsy typewriters and bungling locomotives and tedious bicycles: they are toys compared to the Maxim gun, the submarine torpedo boat. There is nothing in Man's industrial machinery but his greed and sloth: his heart is in his weapons. This marvelous force of Life of which you boast is a force of Death: Man measures his strength by his destructiveness. What is his religion? An excuse for hating ME. What is his law? An excuse for hanging YOU. What is his morality? Gentility! An excuse for consuming without producing. What is his art? An excuse for gloating over pictures of slaughter. What are his politics? Either the worship of a despot because a despot can kill, or parliamentary cockfighting. I spent an evening lately in a certain celebrated legislature, and heard the pot lecturing the kettle for its blackness, and ministers answering questions. When I left I chalked up on the door the old nursery saying — "Ask no questions and you will be told no lies." I bought a six-penny family magazine, and found it full of pictures of young men shooting and stabbing one another. I saw a man die: he was a London brick-layer's laborer with seven children. He left seventeen pounds club money; and his wife spent it all on his funeral and went into the workhouse with the children next day. She would not have spent seven pence on her children's schooling: the law had to force her to let them be taught gratuitously; but on death she spent all she had. Their imagination glows, their energies rise up at the idea of death, these people: they love it; and the more horrible it is the more they enjoy it. Hell is a place far above their comprehension: they derive their notion of it from two of the greatest fools that ever lived, an Italian and an Englishman. The Italian described it as a place of mud, frost, filth, fire, and venomous serpents: all torture. This ass, when he was not lying about me, was maundering about some woman whom he saw once in the street. The Englishman described me as being expelled from Heaven by cannons and gunpowder; and to this day every Briton believes that the whole of his silly story is in the Bible. What else he says I do not know; for it is all in a long poem which neither I nor anyone else ever succeeded in wading through. It is the same in everything. The highest form of literature is the tragedy, a play in which everybody is murdered at the end. In the old chronicles you read of earthquakes and pestilences, and are told that these showed the power and majesty of God and the littleness of Man. Nowadays the chronicles describe battles. In a battle two bodies of men shoot at one another with bullets and explosive shells until one body runs away, when the others chase the fugitives on horseback and cut them to pieces as they fly. And this, the chronicle concludes, shows the greatness and majesty of empires, and the littleness of the vanquished. Over such battles the people run about the streets yelling with delight, and egg their Governments on to spend hundreds of millions of money in the slaughter, whilst the strongest Ministers dare not spend an extra penny in the pound against the poverty and pestilence through which they themselves daily walk. I could give you a thousand instances; but they all come to the same thing: the power that governs the earth is not the power of Life but of Death; and the inner need that has nerved Life to the effort of organizing itself into the human being is not the need for higher life but for a more efficient engine of destruction. The plague, the famine, the earthquake, the tempest were too spasmodic in their action; the tiger and crocodile were too easily satiated and not cruel enough: something more constantly, more ruthlessly, more ingeniously destructive was needed; and that something was Man, the inventor of the rack, the stake, the gallows, and the electrocutor; of the sword and gun; above all, of justice, duty, patriotism and all the other isms by which even those who are clever enough to be humanely disposed are persuaded to become the most destructive of all the destroyers.

DON JUAN: Pshaw! All this is old. Your weak side, my diabolic friend, is that you have always been a gull: you take Man at his own valuation. Nothing would flatter him more than your opinion of him. He loves to think of himself as bold and bad. He is neither one nor the other: he is only a coward. Call him tyrant, murderer, pirate, bully; and he will adore you, and swagger about with the consciousness of having the blood of the old sea kings in his veins. Call him liar and thief; and he will only take an action against you for libel. But call him coward; and he will go mad with rage: he will face death to outface that stinging truth. Man gives every reason for his conduct save one, every excuse for his crimes save one, every plea for his safety save one; and that one is his cowardice. Yet all his civilization is founded on his cowardice, on his abject tameness, which he calls his respectability. There are limits to what a mule or an ass will stand; but Man will suffer himself to be degraded until his vileness becomes so loathsome to his oppressors that they themselves are forced to reform it.

THE DEVIL: Precisely. And these are the creatures in whom you discover what you call a Life Force!

DON JUAN: Yes; for now comes the most surprising part of the whole business.

THE STATUE: What's that?

DON JUAN: Why, that you can make any of these cowards brave by simply putting an idea into his head.

THE STATUE: Stuff! As an old soldier I admit the cowardice: it's as universal as sea sickness, and matters just as little. But that about putting an idea into a man's head is stuff and nonsense. In a battle all you need to make you fight is a little hot blood and the knowledge that it's more dangerous to lose than to win.

DON JUAN: That is perhaps why battles are so useless. But men never really overcome fear until they imagine they are fighting to further a universal purpose — fighting for an idea, as they call it. Why was the Crusader braver than the pirate? Because he fought, not for himself, but for the Cross. What force was it that met him with a valor as reckless as his own? The force of men who fought, not for themselves, but for Islam. They took Spain from us, though we were fighting for our very hearths and homes; but when we, too, fought for that mighty idea, a Catholic Church, we swept them back to Africa.

THE DEVIL: *(Ironically.)* What! You a Catholic, Senor Don Juan! A devotee! My congratulations.

THE STATUE: *(Seriously.)* Come, come! As a soldier, I can listen to nothing against the Church.

DON JUAN: Have no fear, Commander: this idea of a Catholic Church will survive Islam, will survive the Cross, will survive even that vulgar pageant of incompetent schoolboyish gladiators which you call the Army.

THE STATUE: Juan: you will force me to call you to account for this.

DON JUAN: Useless: I cannot fence. Every idea for which Man will die will be a Catholic idea. When the Spaniard learns at last that he is no better than the Saracen, and his prophet no better than Mahomet, he will arise, more Catholic than ever, and die on a barricade across the filthy slum he starves in, for universal liberty and equality.

THE STATUE: Bosh!

DON JUAN: What you call bosh is the only thing men dare die for. Later on, Liberty will not be Catholic enough: men will die for human perfection, to which they will sacrifice all their liberty gladly.

THE DEVIL: Ay: they will never be at a loss for an excuse for killing one another.

DON JUAN: What of that? It is not death that matters, but the fear of death. It is not killing and dying that degrade us, but base living, and accepting the wages and profits of degradation. Better ten dead men than one live slave or his master. Men shall yet rise up, father against son and brother against brother, and kill one another for the great Catholic idea of abolishing slavery.

THE DEVIL: Yes, when the Liberty and Equality of which you prate shall have made free white Christians cheaper in the labor market than by auction at the block.

DON JUAN: Never fear! The white laborer shall have his turn too. But I am not now defending the illusory forms the great ideas take. I am giving you examples of the fact that this creature Man, who in his own selfish affairs is a coward to the backbone, will fight for an idea like a hero. He may be abject as a citizen; but he is dangerous as a fanatic. He can only be enslaved whilst he is spiritually weak enough to listen to reason. I tell you, gentlemen, if you can show a man a piece of what he now calls God's work to do, and what he will later on call by many new names, you can make him entirely reckless of the consequences to himself personally.

ANA: Yes: he shirks all his responsibilities, and leaves his wife to grapple with them.

THE STATUE: Well said, daughter. Do not let him talk you out of your common sense.

THE DEVIL: Alas! Senor Commander, now that we have got on to the subject of Woman, he will talk more than ever. However, I confess it is for me the one supremely interesting subject.

DON JUAN: To a woman, Senora, man's duties and responsibilities begin and end with the task of getting bread for her children. To her, Man is only a means to the end of getting children and rearing them.

ANA: Is that your idea of a woman's mind? I call it cynical and disgusting materialism.

****

from **Major Barbara** (1907)
Act Three

CHARACTERS

> Major Barbara
> Cusins
> Lady Britomart
> Undershaft
> Sarah
> Lomax
> Bilton
> Stephen

[Major Barbara, a devout officer in the Salvation Army, grows disillusioned after the army saves itself from financial difficulties by accepting a donation from her father, an arms manufacturer and successful businessman. In this scene, her father, Undershaft, and her fiancé, Cusins, talk business, much to Barbara's discontent.]

BARBARA: Is the bargain closed, Dolly? Does your soul belong to him now?

CUSINS: No: the price is settled: that is all. The real tug of war is still to come. What about the moral question?

LADY BRITOMART: There is no moral question in the matter at all, Adolphus. You must simply sell cannons and weapons to people whose cause is right and just, and refuse them to foreigners and criminals.

UNDERSHAFT: *(Determinedly.)* No: none of that. You must keep the true faith of an Armorer, or you don't come in here.

CUSINS: What on earth is the true faith of an Armorer?

UNDERSHAFT: To give arms to all men who offer an honest price for them, without respect of persons or principles: to aristocrat and republican, to Nihilist and Tsar, to Capitalist and Socialist, to Protestant and Catholic, to burglar and policeman, to black man white man and yellow man, to all sorts and conditions, all nationalities, all faiths, all follies, all causes and all crimes. The first Undershaft wrote up in his shop IF GOD GAVE THE HAND, LET NOT MAN WITHHOLD THE SWORD. The second wrote up ALL HAVE THE RIGHT TO FIGHT: NONE HAVE THE RIGHT TO JUDGE. The third wrote up TO MAN THE WEAPON: TO HEAVEN THE VICTORY. The fourth had no literary turn; so he did not write up anything; but he sold cannons to Napoleon under the nose of George the Third. The fifth wrote up PEACE SHALL NOT PREVAIL SAVE WITH A SWORD IN HER HAND. The sixth, my master, was the best of all. He wrote up NOTHING IS EVER DONE IN THIS WORLD UNTIL MEN ARE PREPARED TO KILL ONE ANOTHER IF IT IS NOT DONE. After that, there was nothing left for the seventh to say. So he wrote up, simply, UNASHAMED.

CUSINS: My good Machiavelli, I shall certainly write something up on the wall; only, as I shall write it in Greek, you wont be able to read it. But as to your Armorer's faith, if I take my neck out of the noose of my own morality I am not going to put it into the noose of yours. I shall sell cannons to whom I please and refuse them to whom I please. So there!

UNDERSHAFT: From the moment when you become Andrew Undershaft, you will never do as you please again. Don't come here lusting for power, young man.

CUSINS: If power were my aim I should not come here for it. *You* have no power.

UNDERSHAFT: None of my own, certainly.

CUSINS: I have more power than you, more will. You do not drive this place: it drives you. And what drives the place?

UNDERSHAFT: *(Enigmatically.)* A will of which I am a part.

BARBARA: *(Startled.)* Father! Do you know what you are saying; or are you laying a snare for my soul?

CUSINS: Don't listen to his metaphysics, Barbara. The place is driven by the most rascally part of society, the money hunters, the pleasure hunters, the military promotion hunters; and he is their slave.

UNDERSHAFT: Not necessarily. Remember the Armorer's Faith. I will take an order from a good man as cheerfully as from a bad one. If you good people prefer preaching and shirking to buying my weapons and fighting the rascals, don't blame me. I can make cannons: I cannot make courage and conviction. Bah! You tire me, Euripides, with your morality mongering. Ask Barbara: *she* understands. *(He suddenly takes Barbara's hands, and looks powerfully into her eyes.)* Tell him, my love, what power really means.

BARBARA: *(Hypnotized.)* Before I joined the Salvation Army, I was in my own power; and the consequence was that I never knew what to do with myself. When I joined it, I had not time enough for all the things I had to do

UNDERSHAFT: *(Approvingly.)* Just so. And why was that, do you suppose?

BARBARA: Yesterday I should have said, because I was in the power of God. *(She resumes her self-possession, withdrawing her hands from his with a power equal to his own.)* But you came and showed me that I was in the power of Bodger and Undershaft. Today I feel — oh! how can I put into words? Sarah: do you remember the earthquake at Cannes, when we were little children? How little the surprise of the first shock mattered compared to the dread and horror of waiting for the second? That is how I feel in this place today. I stood on the rock I thought eternal; and without a word of warning it reeled and crumbled under me. I was safe with an infinite wisdom watching me, an army marching to Salvation with me; and in a moment, at a stroke of your pen in a cheque book, I stood alone; and the heavens were empty. That was the first shock of the earthquake: I am waiting for the second.

UNDERSHAFT: Come, come, my daughter! Don't make too much of your little tin-pot tragedy. What do we do here when we spend years of work and thought and thousands of pounds of solid cash on a new gun or an aerial battleship that turns out just a hairsbreadth wrong after all? Scrap it. Scrap it without wasting another hour or another pound on it. Well, you have made for yourself something that you call a morality or a religion or what not. It doesn't fit the facts. Well, scrap it. Scrap it and get one that does fit. That is what is wrong with the world at present. It scraps its obsolete steam engines and dynamos; but it won't scrap its old prejudices and its old moralities and its old religions and its old political constitutions. What's the result? In machinery it does very well; but in morals and religion and politics it is working at a loss that brings it nearer bankruptcy every year. Don't persist in that folly. If your old religion broke down yesterday, get a newer and a better one for tomorrow.

BARBARA: Oh how gladly I would take a better one to my soul! But you offer me a worse one. (*Turning on him with sudden vehemence.*) Justify yourself: show me some light through the darkness of this dreadful place, with its beautifully clean workshops, and respectable workmen, and model homes.

UNDERSHAFT: Cleanliness and respectability do not need justification, Barbara: they justify themselves. I see no darkness here, no dreadfulness. In your Salvation shelter I saw poverty, misery, cold and hunger. You gave them bread and treacle and dreams of heaven. I give from thirty shillings a week to twelve thousand a year. They find their own dreams; but I look after the drainage.

BARBARA: And their souls?

UNDERSHAFT: I save their souls just as I saved yours.

BARBARA: (*Revolted.*) *You* saved my soul! What do you mean?

UNDERSHAFT: I fed you and clothed you and housed you. I took care that you should have money enough to live handsomely — more than enough; so that you could be wasteful, careless, generous. That saved your soul from the seven deadly sins.

BARBARA: *(Bewildered.)* The seven deadly sins!

UNDERSHAFT: Yes, the deadly seven. *(Counting on his fingers.)* Food, clothing, firing, rent, taxes, respectability and children. Nothing can lift those seven millstones from Man's neck but money; and the spirit cannot soar until the millstones are lifted. I lifted them from your spirit. I enabled Barbara to become Major Barbara; and I saved her from the crime of poverty.

CUSINS: Do you call poverty a crime?

UNDERSHAFT: The worst of crimes. All the other crimes are virtues beside it: all the other dishonors are chivalry itself by comparison. Poverty blights whole cities; spreads horrible pestilences; strikes dead the very souls of all who come within sight, sound or smell of it. What *you* call crime is nothing: a murder here and a theft there, a blow now and a curse then: what do they matter? They are only the accidents and illnesses of life: there are not fifty genuine professional criminals in London. But there are millions of poor people, abject people, dirty people, ill fed, ill clothed people. They poison us morally and physically: they kill the happiness of society: they force us to do away with our own liberties and to organize unnatural cruelties for fear they should rise against us and drag us down into their abyss. Only fools fear crime: we all fear poverty. Pah! *(Turning on Barbara.)* You talk of your half-saved ruffian in West Ham: you accuse me of dragging his soul back to perdition. Well, bring him to me here; and I will drag his soul back again to salvation for you. Not by words and dreams; but by thirty-eight shillings a week, a sound house in a handsome street, and a permanent job. In three weeks he will have a fancy waistcoat; in three months a tall hat and a chapel sitting; before the end of the year he will shake hands with a duchess at a Primrose League meeting, and join the Conservative Party.

BARBARA: And will he be the better for that?

UNDERSHAFT: You know he will. Don't be a hypocrite, Barbara. He will be better fed, better housed, better clothed, better behaved; and his children will be pounds heavier and bigger. That will be better than an American cloth mattress in a shelter, chopping firewood, eating bread and treacle, and being forced to kneel down from time to time to thank heaven for it: knee drill, I think you call it. It is cheap work converting starving men with a Bible in one hand and a slice of bread in the other. I will undertake to convert West Ham to Mahometanism on the same terms. Try your hand on *my* men: their souls are hungry because their bodies are full.

BARBARA: And leave the east end to starve?

UNDERSHAFT: *(His energetic tone dropping into one of bitter and brooding remembrance.)* I was an east ender. I moralized and starved until one day I swore that I would be a full-fed free man at all costs — that nothing should stop me except a bullet, neither reason nor morals nor the lives of other men. I said "Thou shalt starve ere I starve"; and with that word I became free and great. I was a dangerous man until I had my will: now I am a useful, beneficent, kindly person. That is the history of most self-made millionaires, I fancy. When it is the history of every Englishman we shall have an England worth living in.

LADY BRITOMART: Stop making speeches, Andrew. This is not the place for them.

UNDERSHAFT: *(Punctured.)* My dear: I have no other means of conveying my ideas.

LADY BRITOMART: Your ideas are nonsense. You got on because you were selfish and unscrupulous.

UNDERSHAFT: Not at all. I had the strongest scruples about poverty and starvation. Your moralists are quite unscrupulous about both: they make virtues of them. I had rather be a thief than a pauper. I had rather be a murderer than a slave. I don't want to be either; but if you force the alternative on me, then, by Heaven, I'll choose the braver and more moral one. I hate poverty and slavery worse than any other crimes whatsoever. And let me tell you this. Poverty and slavery have stood up for centuries to your sermons and leading articles: they will not stand up to my machine guns. Don't preach at them: don't reason with them. Kill them.

BARBARA: Killing. Is that your remedy for everything?

UNDERSHAFT: It is the final test of conviction, the only lever strong enough to overturn a social system, the only way of saying Must. Let six hundred and seventy fools loose in the street; and three policemen can scatter them. But huddle them together in a certain house in Westminster; and let them go through certain ceremonies and call themselves certain names until at last they get the courage to kill; and your six hundred and seventy fools become a government. Your pious mob fills up ballot papers and imagines it is governing its masters; but the ballot paper that really governs is the paper that has a bullet wrapped up in it.

CUSINS: That is perhaps why, like most intelligent people, I never vote.

UNDERSHAFT: Vote! Bah! When you vote, you only change the names of the cabinet. When you shoot, you pull down governments, inaugurate new epochs, abolish old orders and set up new. Is that historically true, Mr. Learned Man, or is it not?

CUSINS: It is historically true. I loathe having to admit it. I repudiate your sentiments. I abhor your nature. I defy you in every possible way. Still, it is true. But it ought not to be true.

UNDERSHAFT: Ought, ought, ought, ought, ought! Are you going to spend your life saying ought, like the rest of our moralists? Turn your oughts into shalls, man. Come and make explosives with me. Whatever can blow men up can blow society up. The history of the world is the history of those who had courage enough to embrace this truth. Have you the courage to embrace it, Barbara?

LADY BRITOMART: Barbara, I positively forbid you to listen to your father's abominable wickedness. And you, Adolphus, ought to know better than to go about saying that wrong things are true. What does it matter whether they are true if they are wrong?

UNDERSHAFT: What does it matter whether they are wrong if they are true?

LADY BRITOMART: *(Rising.)* Children: come home instantly. Andrew: I am exceedingly sorry I allowed you to call on us. You are wickeder than ever. Come at once.

BARBARA: *(Shaking her head.)* It's no use running away from wicked people, mamma.

LADY BRITOMART: It is every use. It shows your disapprobation of them.

BARBARA: It does not save them.

LADY BRITOMART: I can see that you are going to disobey me. Sarah: are you coming home or are you not?

SARAH: I daresay it's very wicked of papa to make cannons; but I don't think I shall cut him on that account.

LOMAX: *(Pouring oil on the troubled waters.)* The fact is, you know, there is a certain amount of tosh about this notion of wickedness. It doesn't work. You must look at facts. Not that I would say a word in favor of anything wrong; but then, you see, all sorts of chaps are always doing all sorts of things; and we have to fit them in somehow, don't you know. What I mean is that you can't go cutting everybody; and that's about what it comes to. *(Their rapt attention to his eloquence makes him nervous.)* Perhaps I don't make myself clear.

LADY BRITOMART: You are lucidity itself, Charles. Because Andrew is successful and has plenty of money to give to Sarah, you will flatter him and encourage him in his wickedness.

LOMAX: *(Unruffled.)* Well, where the carcase is, there will the eagles be gathered, don't you know. *(To Undershaft.)* Eh? What?

UNDERSHAFT: Precisely. By the way, *may* I call you Charles?

LOMAX: Delighted. Cholly is the usual ticket.

UNDERSHAFT: *(To Lady Britomart.)* Biddy —

LADY BRITOMART: *(Violently.)* Don't dare call me Biddy. Charles Lomax: you are a fool. Adolphus Cusins: you are a Jesuit. Stephen: you are a prig. Barbara: you are a lunatic. Andrew: you are a vulgar tradesman. Now you all know my opinion; and *my* conscience is clear, at all events. *(She sits down again with a vehemence that almost wrecks the chair.)*

UNDERSHAFT: My dear: you are the incarnation of morality. *(She snorts.)* Your conscience is clear and your duty done when you have called everybody names. Come, Euripides! it is getting late; and we all want to get home. Make up your mind.

CUSINS: Understand this, you old demon —

LADY BRITOMART: Adolphus!

UNDERSHAFT: Let him alone, Biddy. Proceed, Euripides.

CUSINS: You have me in a horrible dilemma. I want Barbara.

UNDERSHAFT: Like all young men, you greatly exaggerate the difference between one young woman and another.

BARBARA: Quite true, Dolly.

CUSINS: I also want to avoid being a rascal.

UNDERSHAFT*: (With biting contempt.)* You lust for personal righteousness, for self-approval, for what you call a good conscience, for what Barbara calls salvation, for what I call patronizing people who are not so lucky as yourself.

CUSINS: I do not: all the poet in me recoils from being a good man. But there are things in me that I must reckon with: pity —

UNDERSHAFT: Pity! The scavenger of misery.

CUSINS: Well, love.

UNDERSHAFT: I know. You love the needy and the outcast: you love the oppressed races, the negro, the Indian ryot, the Pole, the Irishman. Do you love the Japanese? Do you love the Germans? Do you love the English?

CUSINS: No. Every true Englishman detests the English. We are the wickedest nation on earth; and our success is a moral horror.

UNDERSHAFT: That is what comes of your gospel of love, is it?

CUSINS: May I not love even my father-in-law?

UNDERSHAFT: Who wants your love, man? By what right do you take the liberty of offering it to me? I will have your due heed and respect, or I will kill you. But your love. Damn your impertinence!

CUSINS: *(Grinning.)* I may not be able to control my affections, Mac.

UNDERSHAFT: You are fencing, Euripides. You are weakening: your grip is slipping. Come! try your last weapon. Pity and love have broken in your hand: forgiveness is still left.

CUSINS: No: forgiveness is a beggar's refuge. I am with you there: we must pay our debts.

UNDERSHAFT: Well said. Come! you will suit me. Remember the words of Plato.

CUSINS: *(Starting.)* Plato! You dare quote Plato to me!

UNDERSHAFT: Plato says, my friend, that society cannot be saved until either the Professors of Greek take to making gunpowder, or else the makers of gunpowder become Professors of Greek.

CUSINS: Oh, tempter, cunning tempter!

UNDERSHAFT: Come! Choose, man, choose.

CUSINS: But perhaps Barbara will not marry me if I make the wrong choice.

BARBARA: Perhaps not.

CUSINS: *(Desperately perplexed.)* You hear!

BARBARA: Father: do you love nobody?

UNDERSHAFT: I love my best friend.

LADY BRITOMART: And who is that, pray?

UNDERSHAFT: My bravest enemy. That is the man who keeps me up to the mark.

CUSINS: You know, the creature is really a sort of poet in his way. Suppose he is a great man, after all!

UNDERSHAFT: Suppose you stop talking and make up your mind, my young friend.

CUSINS: But you are driving me against my nature. I hate war.

UNDERSHAFT: Hatred is the coward's revenge for being intimidated. Dare you make war on war? Here are the means: my friend Mr. Lomax is sitting on them.

LOMAX: *(Springing up.)* Oh I say! You don't mean that this thing is loaded, do you? My ownest: come off it.

SARAH: *(Sitting placidly on the shell.)* If I am to be blown up, the more thoroughly it is done the better. Don't fuss, Cholly.

LOMAX: *(To Undershaft, strongly remonstrant.)* Your own daughter, you know.

UNDERSHAFT: So I see. *(To Cusins.)* Well, my friend, may we expect you here at six tomorrow morning?

CUSINS: *(Firmly.)* Not on any account. I will see the whole establishment blown up with its own dynamite before I will get up at five. My hours are healthy, rational hours: eleven to five.

UNDERSHAFT: Come when you please: before a week you will come at six and stay until I turn you out for the sake of your health. *(Calling.)* Bilton! *(He turns to Lady Britomart, who rises.)* My dear: let us leave these two young people to themselves for a moment. *(Bilton comes from the shed.)* I am going to take you through the gun cotton shed.

BILTON: *(Barring the way.)* You can't take anything explosive in here, sir.

LADY BRITOMART: What do you mean? Are you alluding to me?

BILTON: *(Unmoved.)* No, ma'am. Mr. Undershaft has the other gentleman's matches in his pocket.

LADY BRITOMART: *(Abruptly.)* Oh! I beg your pardon. *(She goes into the shed.)*

UNDERSHAFT: Quite right, Bilton, quite right: here you are. *(He gives Bilton the box of matches.)* Come, Stephen. Come, Charles. Bring Sarah. *(He passes into the shed.)*

(Bilton opens the box and deliberately drops the matches into the fire-bucket.)

LOMAX: Oh I say! *(Bilton stolidly hands him the empty box.)* Infernal nonsense! Pure scientific ignorance! *(He goes in.)*

SARAH: Am I all right, Bilton?

BILTON: You'll have to put on list slippers miss: that's all. We've got 'em inside. *(She goes in.)*

STEPHEN: *(Very seriously to Cusins.)* Dolly, old fellow, think. Think before you decide. Do you feel that you are a sufficiently practical man? It is a huge undertaking, an enormous responsibility. All this mass of business will be Greek to you.

CUSINS: Oh, I think it will be much less difficult than Greek.

STEPHEN: Well, I just want to say this before I leave you to yourselves. Don't let anything I have said about right and wrong prejudice you against this great chance in life. I have satisfied myself that the business is one of the highest character and a credit to our country. *(Emotionally.)* I am very proud of my father. I — *(Unable to proceed, he presses Cusins' hand and goes hastily into the shed, followed by Bilton.)*

(Barbara and Cusins, left alone together, look at one another silently.)

CUSINS: Barbara: I am going to accept this offer.

BARBARA: I thought you would.

CUSINS: You understand, don't you, that I had to decide without consulting you. If I had thrown the burden of the choice on you, you would sooner or later have despised me for it.

BARBARA: Yes: I did not want you to sell your soul for me any more than for this inheritance.

CUSINS: It is not the sale of my soul that troubles me: I have sold it too often to care about that. I have sold it for a professorship. I have sold it for an income. I have sold it to escape being imprisoned for refusing to pay taxes for hangmen's ropes and unjust wars and things that I abhor. What is all-human conduct but the daily and hourly sale of our souls for trifles? What I am now selling it for is neither money nor position nor comfort, but for reality and for power.

BARBARA: You know that you will have no power, and that he has none.

CUSINS: I know. It is not for myself alone. I want to make power for the world.

BARBARA: I want to make power for the world too; but it must be spiritual power.

CUSINS: I think all power is spiritual: these cannons will not go off by themselves. I have tried to make spiritual power by teaching Greek. But the world can never be really touched by a dead language and a dead civilization. The people must have power; and the people cannot have Greek. Now the power that is made here can be wielded by all men.

BARBARA: Power to burn women's houses down and kill their sons and tear their husbands to pieces.

CUSINS: You cannot have power for good without having power for evil too. Even mother's milk nourishes murderers as well as heroes. This power which only tears men's bodies to pieces has never been so horribly abused as the intellectual power, the imaginative power, the poetic, religious power than can enslave men's souls. As a teacher of Greek I gave the intellectual man weapons against the common man. I now want to give the common man weapons against the intellectual man. I love the common people. I want to arm them against the lawyer, the doctor, the priest, the literary man, the professor, the artist, and the politician, who, once in authority, are the most dangerous, disastrous, and tyrannical of all the fools, rascals, and impostors. I want a democratic power strong enough to force the intellectual oligarchy to use its genius for the general good or else perish

BARBARA: Is there no higher power than that? *(Pointing to the shell.)*

CUSINS: Yes: but that power can destroy the higher powers just as a tiger can destroy a man: therefore man must master that power first. I admitted this when the Turks and Greeks were last at war. My best pupil went out to fight for Hellas. My parting gift to him was not a copy of Plato's Republic, but a revolver and a hundred Undershaft cartridges. The blood of every Turk he shot — if he shot any — is on my head as well as on Undershaft's. That act committed me to this place forever. Your father's challenge has beaten me. Dare I make war on war? I dare. I must. I will. And now, is it all over between us?

BARBARA: *(Touched by his evident dread of her answer.)* Silly baby Dolly! How could it be?

CUSINS: *(Overjoyed.)* Then you — you — you — Oh for my drum! *(He flourishes imaginary drumsticks.)*

BARBARA: *(Angered by his levity.)* Take care, Dolly, take care. Oh, if only I could get away from you and from father and from it all! If I could have the wings of a dove and fly away to heaven!

CUSINS: And leave me!

BARBARA: Yes, you, and all the other naughty mischievous children of men. But I cant. I was happy in the Salvation Army for a moment. I escaped from the world into a paradise of enthusiasm and prayer and soul saving; but the moment our money ran short, it all came back to Bodger: it was he who saved our people: he, and the Prince of Darkness, my papa. Undershaft and Bodger: their hands stretch everywhere: when we feed a starving fellow creature, it is with their bread, because there is no other bread; when we tend the sick, it is in the hospitals they endow; if we turn from the churches they build, we must kneel on the stones of the streets they pave. As long as that lasts, there is no getting away from them. Turning our backs on Bodger and Undershaft is turning our backs on life.

CUSINS: I thought you were determined to turn your back on the wicked side of life.

BARBARA: There is no wicked side: life is all one. And I never wanted to shirk my share in whatever evil must be endured, whether it be sin or suffering. I wish I could cure you of middle-class ideas, Dolly.

CUSINS: *(Gasping.)* Middle cl — ! A snub! A social snub to me! from the daughter of a foundling!

BARBARA: That is why I have no class, Dolly: I come straight out of the heart of the whole people. If I were middle-class I should turn my back on my father's business; and we should both live in an artistic drawing room, with you reading the reviews in one corner, and I in the other at the piano, playing Schumann: both very superior persons, and neither of us a bit of use. Sooner than that, I would sweep out the guncotton shed, or be one of Bodger's barmaids. Do you know what would have happened if you had refused papa's offer?

CUSINS: I wonder!

BARBARA: I should have given you up and married the man who accepted it. After all, my dear old mother has more sense than any of you. I felt like her when I saw this place — felt that I must have it — that never, never, never could I let it go; only she thought it was the houses and the kitchen ranges and the linen and china, when it was really all the human souls to be saved: not weak souls in starved bodies, crying with gratitude for a scrap of bread and treacle, but full-fed, quarrelsome, snobbish, uppish creatures, all standing on their little rights and dignities, and thinking that my father ought to be greatly obliged to them for making so much money for him — and so he ought. That is where salvation is really wanted. My father shall never throw it in my teeth again that my converts were bribed with bread. *(She is transfigured.)* I have got rid of the bribe of bread. I have got rid of the bribe of heaven. Let God's work be done for its own sake: the work he had to create us to do because it cannot be done except by living men and women. When I die, let him be in my debt, not I in his; and let me forgive him as becomes a woman of my rank.

CUSINS: Then the way of life lies through the factory of death?

BARBARA: Yes, through the raising of hell to heaven and of man to God, through the unveiling of an eternal light in the Valley of The

Shadow. *(Seizing him with both hands.)* Oh, did you think my courage would never come back? Did you believe that I was a deserter? That I, who have stood in the streets, and taken my people to my heart, and talked of the holiest and greatest things with them, could ever turn back and chatter foolishly to fashionable people about nothing in a drawing room? Never, never, never, never: Major Barbara will die with the colors. Oh! And I have my dear little Dolly boy still; and he has found me my place and my work. Glory Hallelujah! *(She kisses him.)*

CUSINS: My dearest: consider my delicate health. I cannot stand as much happiness as you can.

BARBARA: Yes: it is not easy work being in love with me, is it? But it's good for you. *(She runs to the shed, and calls, childlike)* Mamma! Mamma! *(Bilton comes out of the shed, followed by Undershaft.)* I want Mamma.

UNDERSHAFT: She is taking off her list slippers, dear. *(He passes on to Cusins.)* Well? What does she say?

CUSINS: She has gone right up into the skies.

LADY BRITOMART: *(Coming from the shed and stopping on the steps, obstructing Sarah, who follows with Lomax. Barbara clutches like a baby at her mother's skirt.)* Barbara: when will you learn to be independent and to act and think for yourself? I know as well as possible what that cry of "Mamma, Mamma," means. Always running to me!

SARAH: *(Touching Lady Britomart's ribs with her finger tips and imitating a bicycle horn.)* Pip! pip!

LADY BRITOMART: *(Highly indignant.)* How dare you say Pip! Pip! to me, Sarah? You are both very naughty children. What do you want, Barbara?

BARBARA: I want a house in the village to live in with Dolly. *(Dragging at the skirt.)* Come and tell me which one to take.

UNDERSHAFT: *(To Cusins.)* Six o'clock tomorrow morning, my young friend.

****

from **Pygmalion** (1916)
Act Five

CHARACTERS

Professor Higgins
Eliza Doolittle
Mrs. Higgins

[Perhaps the most famous Shaw play, Pygmalion is about the cockney-flower-girl-turned-society-lady Eliza Doolittle. In this scene, Henry Higgins, the professor of phonetics responsible for Eliza Doolittle's transformation, struggles as he has to let go of his creation.]

HIGGINS: Well, Eliza, you've had a bit of your own back, as you call it. Have you had enough? And are you going to be reasonable? Or do you want any more?

ELIZA: You want me back only to pick up your slippers and put up with your tempers and fetch and carry for you.

HIGGINS: I haven't said I wanted you back at all.

ELIZA: Oh, indeed. Then what are we talking about?

HIGGINS: About you, not about me. If you come back I shall treat you just as I have always treated you. I can't change my nature; and I don't intend to change my manners. My manners are exactly the same as Colonel Pickering's.

ELIZA: That's not true. He treats a flower girl as if she was a duchess.

HIGGINS: And I treat a duchess as if she was a flower girl.

ELIZA: I see. *(She turns away composedly, and sits on the ottoman, facing the window.)* The same to everybody.

HIGGINS: Just so.

ELIZA: Like father.

HIGGINS: *(Grinning, a little taken down.)* Without accepting the comparison at all points, Eliza, it's quite true that your father is not a snob, and that he will be quite at home in any station of life to which his eccentric destiny may call him. *(Seriously.)* The great secret, Eliza, is not having bad manners or good manners or any other particular sort of manners, but having the same manner for all human souls: in short, behaving as if you were in Heaven, where there are no third-class carriages, and one soul is as good as another.

ELIZA: Amen. You are a born preacher.

HIGGINS: *(Irritated.)* The question is not whether I treat you rudely, but whether you ever heard me treat anyone else better.

ELIZA: *(With sudden sincerity.)* I don't care how you treat me. I don't mind your swearing at me. I don't mind a black eye: I've had one before this. But *(Standing up and facing him.)* I won't be passed over.

HIGGINS: Then get out of my way; for I won't stop for you. You talk about me as if I were a motor bus.

ELIZA: So you are a motor bus: all bounce and go, and no consideration for anyone. But I can do without you: don't think I can't.

HIGGINS: I know you can. I told you, you could.

ELIZA: *(Wounded, getting away from him to the other side of the ottoman with her face to the hearth.)* I know you did, you brute. You wanted to get rid of me.

HIGGINS: Liar.

ELIZA: Thank you. *(She sits down with dignity.)*

HIGGINS: You never asked yourself, I suppose, whether I could do without YOU.

ELIZA: *(Earnestly.)* Don't you try to get round me. You'll HAVE to do without me.

HIGGINS: *(Arrogant.)* I can do without anybody. I have my own soul: my own spark of divine fire. But *(With sudden humility.)* I shall miss you. *(He sits down near her on the ottoman.)* Eliza. I have learnt something from your idiotic notions: I confess that humbly and gratefully. And I have grown accustomed to your voice and appearance. I like them, rather.

ELIZA: Well, you have both of them on your gramophone and in your book of photographs. When you feel lonely without me, you can turn the machine on. It's got no feelings to hurt.

HIGGINS: I can't turn your soul on. Leave me those feelings; and you can take away the voice and the face. They are not you.

ELIZA: Oh, you ARE a devil. You can twist the heart in a girl as easy as some could twist her arms to hurt her. Mrs. Pearce warned me. Time and again she has wanted to leave you; and you always got round her at the last minute. And you don't care a bit for her. And you don't care a bit for me.

HIGGINS: I care for life, for humanity; and you are a part of it that has come my way and been built into my house. What more can you or anyone ask?

ELIZA: I won't care for anybody that doesn't care for me.

HIGGINS: Commercial principles, Eliza. Like (*Reproducing her Covent Garden pronunciation with professional exactness.*) s'yollin voylets (*Selling violets.*), isn't it?

ELIZA: Don't sneer at me. It's mean to sneer at me.

HIGGINS: I have never sneered in my life. Sneering doesn't become either the human face or the human soul. I am expressing my righteous contempt for Commercialism. I don't and won't trade in affection. You call me a brute because you couldn't buy a claim on me by fetching my slippers and finding my spectacles. You were a fool: I think a woman fetching a man's slippers is a disgusting sight: did I ever fetch YOUR slippers? I think a good deal more of you for throwing them in my face. No use slaving for me and then saying you want to be cared for: who cares for a slave? If you come back, come back for the sake of good fellowship; for you'll get nothing else. You've had a thousand times as much out of me as I have out of you; and if you dare to set up your little dog's tricks of fetching and carrying slippers against my creation of a Duchess Eliza, I'll slam the door in your silly face.

ELIZA: What did you do it for if you didn't care for me?

HIGGINS: *(Heartily.)* Why, because it was my job.

ELIZA: You never thought of the trouble it would make for me.

HIGGINS: Would the world ever have been made if its maker had been afraid of making trouble? Making life means making trouble. There's only one way of escaping trouble; and that's killing things. Cowards, you notice, are always shrieking to have troublesome people killed.

ELIZA: I'm no preacher: I don't notice things like that. I notice that you don't notice me.

HIGGINS: *(Jumping up and walking about intolerantly.)* Eliza: you're an idiot. I waste the treasures of my Miltonic mind by spreading them before you. Once for all, understand that I go my way and do my work without caring two pence what happens to either of us. I am not intimidated, like your father and your stepmother. So you can come back or go to the devil: which you please.

ELIZA: What am I to come back for?

HIGGINS: *(Bouncing up on his knees on the ottoman and leaning over it to her.)* For the fun of it. That's why I took you on.

ELIZA: *(With averted face.)* And you may throw me out tomorrow if I don't do everything you want me to?

HIGGINS: Yes; and you may walk out tomorrow if I don't do everything YOU want me to.

ELIZA: And live with my stepmother?

HIGGINS: Yes, or sell flowers.

ELIZA: Oh! if I only COULD go back to my flower basket! I should be independent of both you and father and all the world! Why did you take my independence from me? Why did I give it up? I'm a slave now, for all my fine clothes.

HIGGINS: Not a bit. I'll adopt you as my daughter and settle money on you if you like. Or would you rather marry Pickering?

ELIZA: *(Looking fiercely round at him.)* I wouldn't marry YOU if you asked me; and you're nearer my age than what he is.

HIGGINS: *(Gently.)* Than he is: not "than what he is."

ELIZA: *(Losing her temper and rising.)* I'll talk as I like. You're not my teacher now.

HIGGINS: *(Reflectively.)* I don't suppose Pickering would, though. He's as confirmed an old bachelor as I am.

ELIZA: That's not what I want; and don't you think it. I've always had chaps enough wanting me that way. Freddy Hill writes to me twice and three times a day, sheets and sheets.

HIGGINS: *(Disagreeably surprised.)* Damn his impudence! *(He recoils and finds himself sitting on his heels.)*

ELIZA: He has a right to if he likes, poor lad. And he does love me.

HIGGINS: *(Getting off the ottoman.)* You have no right to encourage him.

ELIZA: Every girl has a right to be loved.

HIGGINS: What! By fools like that?

ELIZA: Freddy's not a fool. And if he's weak and poor and wants me, may be he'd make me happier than my betters that bully me and don't want me.

HIGGINS: Can he MAKE anything of you? That's the point.

ELIZA: Perhaps I could make something of him. But I never thought of us making anything of one another; and you never think of anything else. I only want to be natural.

HIGGINS: In short, you want me to be as infatuated about you as Freddy? Is that it?

ELIZA: No I don't. That's not the sort of feeling I want from you. And don't you be too sure of yourself or of me. I could have been a bad girl if I'd liked. I've seen more of some things than you, for all your learning. Girls like me can drag gentlemen down to make love to them easy enough. And they wish each other dead the next minute.

HIGGINS: Of course they do. Then what in thunder are we quarrelling about?

ELIZA: *(Much troubled.)* I want a little kindness. I know I'm a common ignorant girl, and you a book-learned gentleman; but I'm not dirt under your feet. What I done *(Correcting herself.)* what I did was not for the dresses and the taxis: I did it because we were pleasant together and I come — came — to care for you; not to want you to make love to me, and not forgetting the difference between us, but more friendly like.

HIGGINS: Well, of course. That's just how I feel. And how Pickering feels. Eliza: you're a fool.

ELIZA: That's not a proper answer to give me. *(She sinks on the chair at the writing-table in tears.)*

HIGGINS: It's all you'll get until you stop being a common idiot. If you're going to be a lady, you'll have to give up feeling neglected if the men you know don't spend half their time sniveling over you and the other half giving you black eyes. If you can't stand the coldness of my sort of life, and the strain of it, go back to the gutter. Work till you are more a brute than a human being; and then cuddle and squabble and drink till you fall asleep. Oh, it's a fine life, the life of the gutter. It's real: it's warm: it's violent: you can feel it through the thickest skin: you can taste it and smell it without any training or any work. Not like Science and Literature and Classical Music and Philosophy and Art. You find me cold, unfeeling, selfish, don't you? Very well: be off with you to the sort of people you like. Marry some sentimental hog or other with lots of money, and a thick pair of lips to kiss you with and a thick pair of boots to kick you with. If you can't appreciate what you've got, you'd better get what you can appreciate.

ELIZA: *(Desperate.)* Oh, you are a cruel tyrant. I can't talk to you: you turn everything against me: I'm always in the wrong. But you know very well all the time that you're nothing but a bully. You know I can't go back to the gutter, as you call it, and that I have no real friends in the world but you and the Colonel. You know well I couldn't bear to live with a low common man after you two; and it's wicked and cruel of you to insult me by pretending I could. You think I must go back to Wimpole Street because I have nowhere else to go but father's. But don't you be too sure that you have me under your feet to be trampled on and talked down. I'll marry Freddy, I will, as soon as he's able to support me.

HIGGINS: *(Sitting down beside her.)* Rubbish! You shall marry an ambassador. You shall marry the Governor-General of India or the Lord-Lieutenant of Ireland, or somebody who wants a deputy-queen. I'm not going to have my masterpiece thrown away on Freddy.

ELIZA: You think I like you to say that. But I haven't forgot what you said a minute ago; and I won't be coaxed round as if I was a baby or a puppy. If I can't have kindness, I'll have independence.

HIGGINS: Independence? That's middle class blasphemy. We are all dependent on one another, every soul of us on earth.

ELIZA: *(Rising determinedly.)* I'll let you see whether I'm dependent on you. If you can preach, I can teach. I'll go and be a teacher.

HIGGINS: What'll you teach, in heaven's name?

ELIZA: What you taught me. I'll teach phonetics.

HIGGINS: Ha! Ha! Ha!

ELIZA: I'll offer myself as an assistant to Professor Nepean.

HIGGINS: *(Rising in a fury.)* What! That impostor! that humbug! that toadying ignoramus! Teach him my methods! my discoveries! You take one step in his direction and I'll wring your neck. *(He lays hands on her.)* Do you hear?

ELIZA: *(Defiantly nonresistant.)* Wring away. What do I care? I knew you'd strike me some day. *(He lets her go, stamping with rage at having forgotten himself, and recoils so hastily that he stumbles back into his seat on the ottoman.)* Aha! Now I know how to deal with you. What a fool I was not to think of it before! You can't take away the knowledge you gave me. You said I had a finer ear than you. And I can be civil and kind to people, which is more than you can. Aha! That's done you, Henry Higgins, it has. Now I don't care that *(Snapping her fingers.)* for your bullying and your big talk. I'll advertize it in the papers that your duchess is only a flower girl that you taught, and that she'll teach anybody to be a duchess just the same in six months for a thousand guineas. Oh, when I think of myself crawling under your feet and being trampled on and called names, when all the time I had only to lift up my finger to be as good as you, I could just kick myself.

HIGGINS: *(Wondering at her.)* You damned impudent slut, you! But it's better than sniveling; better than fetching slippers and finding spectacles, isn't it? *(Rising.)* By George, Eliza, I said I'd make a woman of you; and I have. I like you like this.

ELIZA: Yes: you turn round and make up to me now that I'm not afraid of you, and can do without you.

HIGGINS: Of course I do, you little fool. Five minutes ago you were like a millstone round my neck. Now you're a tower of strength: a consort battleship. You and I and Pickering will be three old bachelors together instead of only two men and a silly girl. *(Mrs. Higgins returns, dressed for the wedding. Eliza instantly becomes cool and elegant.)*

MRS. HIGGINS: The carriage is waiting, Eliza. Are you ready?

ELIZA: Quite. Is the Professor coming?

MRS. HIGGINS: Certainly not. He can't behave himself in church. He makes remarks out loud all the time on the clergyman's pronunciation.

ELIZA: Then I shall not see you again, Professor. Good-bye. *(She goes to the door.)*

MRS. HIGGINS: *(Coming to Higgins.)* Good-bye, dear.

HIGGINS: Good-bye, mother. *(He is about to kiss her, when he recollects something.)* Oh, by the way, Eliza, order a ham and a Stilton cheese, will you? And buy me a pair of reindeer gloves, number eights, and a tie to match that new suit of mine, at Eale & Binman's. You can choose the color. *(His cheerful, careless, vigorous voice shows that he is incorrigible.)*

ELIZA: *(Disdainfully.)* Buy them yourself. *(She sweeps out.)*

MRS. HIGGINS: I'm afraid you've spoiled that girl, Henry. But never mind, dear: I'll buy you the tie and gloves.

HIGGINS: *(Sunnily.)* Oh, don't bother. She'll buy 'em all right enough. Good-bye. *(They kiss.)*

(Mrs. Higgins runs out. Higgins, left alone, rattles his cash in his pocket; chuckles; and disports himself in a highly self-satisfied manner.)

****

from **Heartbreak House** (1919)
Act Three

CHARACTERS

Hector
Mazzini
Ellie
Lady Utterword
Captain Shotover
Nurse Guinness
The Burglar
Hesione
Mrs. Hushabye
Randall

[Shaw wrote *Heartbreak House* in part as a reaction to World War I and the disappointment and destruction it brought to Europe. In this play, a family gathers for a dinner party at Captain Shotover's house. The party quickly turns dark and sour. In this final scene, doom and destruction are set against farce and false hope.]

HECTOR: *(Impatiently.)* How is all this going to end?

MAZZINI: It won't end, Mr. Hushabye. Life doesn't end: it goes on.

ELLIE: Oh, it can't go on forever. I'm always expecting something. I don't know what it is; but life must come to a point sometime.

LADY UTTERWORD: The point for a young woman of your age is a baby.

HECTOR: Yes, but, damn it, I have the same feeling; and I can't have a baby.

LADY UTTERWORD: By deputy, Hector.

HECTOR: But I have children. All that is over and done with for me: and yet I too feel that this can't last. We sit here talking, and leave everything to Mangan and to chance and to the devil. Think of the powers of destruction that Mangan and his mutual admiration gang wield! It's madness: it's like giving a torpedo to a badly brought up child to play at earthquakes with.

MAZZINI: I know. I used often to think about that when I was young.

HECTOR: Think! What's the good of thinking about it? Why didn't you do something?

MAZZINI: But I did. I joined societies and made speeches and wrote pamphlets. That was all I could do. But, you know, though the people in the societies thought they knew more than Mangan, most of them wouldn't have joined if they had known as much. You see they had never had any money to handle or any men to manage. Every year I expected a revolution, or some frightful smash-up: it seemed impossible that we could blunder and muddle on any longer. But nothing happened, except, of course, the usual poverty and crime and drink that we are used to. Nothing ever does happen. It's amazing how well we get along, all things considered.

LADY UTTERWORD: Perhaps somebody cleverer than you and Mr. Mangan was at work all the time.

MAZZINI: Perhaps so. Though I was brought up not to believe in anything, I often feel that there is a great deal to be said for the theory of an over-ruling Providence, after all.

LADY UTTERWORD: Providence! I meant Hastings.

MAZZINI: Oh, I beg your pardon, Lady Utterword.

CAPTAIN SHOTOVER: Every drunken skipper trusts to Providence. But one of the ways of Providence with drunken skippers is to run them on the rocks.

MAZZINI: Very true, no doubt, at sea. But in politics, I assure you, they only run into jellyfish. Nothing happens.

CAPTAIN SHOTOVER: At sea nothing happens to the sea. Nothing happens to the sky. The sun comes up from the east and goes down to the west. The moon grows from a sickle to an arc lamp, and comes later and later until she is lost in the light as other things are lost in the darkness. After the typhoon, the flying-fish glitter in the sunshine like birds. It's amazing how they get along, all things considered. Nothing happens, except something not worth mentioning.

ELLIE: What is that, O Captain, O my captain?

CAPTAIN SHOTOVER: *(Savagely.)* Nothing but the smash of the drunken skipper's ship on the rocks, the splintering of her rotten timbers, the tearing of her rusty plates, the drowning of the crew like rats in a trap.

ELLIE: Moral: don't take rum.

CAPTAIN SHOTOVER: *(Vehemently.)* That is a lie, child. Let a man drink ten barrels of rum a day, he is not a drunken skipper until he is a drifting skipper. Whilst he can lay his course and stand on his bridge and steer it, he is no drunkard. It is the man who lies drinking in his bunk and trusts to Providence that I call the drunken skipper, though he drank nothing but the waters of the River Jordan.

ELLIE: Splendid! And you haven't had a drop for an hour. You see you don't need it: your own spirit is not dead.

CAPTAIN SHOTOVER: Echoes: nothing but echoes. The last shot was fired years ago.

HECTOR: And this ship that we are all in? This soul's prison we call England?

CAPTAIN SHOTOVER: The captain is in his bunk, drinking bottled ditch-water; and the crew is gambling in the forecastle. She will strike and sink and split. Do you think the laws of God will be suspended in favor of England because you were born in it?

HECTOR: Well, I don't mean to be drowned like a rat in a trap. I still have the will to live. What am I to do?

CAPTAIN SHOTOVER: Do? Nothing simpler. Learn your business as an Englishman.

HECTOR: And what may my business as an Englishman be, pray?

CAPTAIN SHOTOVER: Navigation. Learn it and live; or leave it and be damned.

ELLIE: Quiet, quiet: you'll tire yourself.

MAZZINI: I thought all that once, Captain; but I assure you nothing will happen.

(A dull distant explosion is heard.)

HECTOR: *(Starting up.)* What was that?

CAPTAIN SHOTOVER: Something happening. *(He blows his whistle.)* Breakers ahead!

(The light goes out.)

HECTOR: *(Furiously.)* Who put that light out? Who dared put that light out?

NURSE GUINNESS: *(Running in from the house to the middle of the Esplanade.)* I did, sir. The police have telephoned to say we'll be summoned if we don't put that light out: it can be seen for miles.

HECTOR: It shall be seen for a hundred miles. *(He dashes into the house.)*

NURSE GUINNESS: The Rectory is nothing but a heap of bricks, they say. Unless we can give the Rector a bed he has nowhere to lay his head this night.

CAPTAIN SHOTOVER: The Church is on the rocks, breaking up. I told him it would unless it headed for God's open sea.

NURSE GUINNESS: And you are all to go down to the cellars.

CAPTAIN SHOTOVER: Go there yourself, you and all the crew. Batten down the hatches.

NURSE GUINNESS: And hide beside the coward I married! I'll go on the roof first. *(The lamp lights up again.)* There! Mr. Hushabye's turned it on again.

THE BURGLAR: *(Hurrying in and appealing to Nurse Guinness.)* Here: where's the way to that gravel pit? The boot-boy says there's a cave in the gravel pit. Them cellars is no use. Where's the gravel pit, Captain?

NURSE GUINNESS: Go straight on past the flagstaff until you fall into it and break your dirty neck. *(She pushes him contemptuously towards the flagstaff, and herself goes to the foot of the hammock and waits there, as it were by Ariadne's cradle.)*

(Another and louder explosion is heard. The burglar stops and stands trembling.)

ELLIE: *(Rising.)* That was nearer.

CAPTAIN SHOTOVER: The next one will get us. *(He rises.)* Stand by, all hands, for judgment.

THE BURGLAR: Oh my Lordy God! *(He rushes away frantically past the flagstaff into the gloom.)*

MRS. HUSHABYE: *(Emerging panting from the darkness.)* Who was that running away? *(She comes to Ellie.)* Did you hear the explosions? And the sound in the sky: it's splendid: it's like an orchestra: it's like Beethoven.

ELLIE: By thunder, Hesione: it is Beethoven. *(She and Hesione throw themselves into one another's arms in wild excitement. The light increases.)*

MAZZINI: *(Anxiously.)* The light is getting brighter.

NURSE GUINNESS: *(Looking up at the house.)* It's Mr. Hushabye turning on all the lights in the house and tearing down the curtains.

RANDALL: *(Rushing in in his pyjamas, distractedly waving a flute.)* Ariadne, my soul, my precious, go down to the cellars: I beg and implore you, go down to the cellars!

LADY UTTERWORD: *(Quite composed in her hammock.)* The governor's wife in the cellars with the servants! Really, Randall!

RANDALL: But what shall I do if you are killed?

LADY UTTERWORD: You will probably be killed, too, Randall. Now play your flute to show that you are not afraid; and be good. Play us "Keep the Home Fires Burning."

NURSE GUINNESS: *(Grimly.)* THEY'LL keep the home fires burning for us: them up there.

RANDALL: *(Having tried to play.)* My lips are trembling. I can't get a sound.

MAZZINI: I hope poor Mangan is safe.

MRS. HUSHABYE: He is hiding in the cave in the gravel pit.

CAPTAIN SHOTOVER: My dynamite drew him there. It is the hand of God.

HECTOR: *(Returning from the house and striding across to his former place.)* There is not half light enough. We should be blazing to the skies.

ELLIE: *(Tense with excitement.)* Set fire to the house, Marcus.

MRS. HUSHABYE. My house! No.

HECTOR: I thought of that; but it would not be ready in time.

CAPTAIN SHOTOVER: The judgment has come. Courage will not save you; but it will show that your souls are still live.

MRS. HUSHABYE. Sh-sh! Listen: do you hear it now? It's magnificent.

(They all turn away from the house and look up, listening.)

HECTOR: *(Gravely.)* Miss Dunn, you can do no good here. We of this house are only moths flying into the candle. You had better go down to the cellar.

ELLIE: *(Scornfully.)* I don't think.

MAZZINI: Ellie, dear, there is no disgrace in going to the cellar. An officer would order his soldiers to take cover. Mr. Hushabye is behaving like an amateur. Mangan and the burglar are acting very sensibly; and it is they who will survive.

ELLIE: Let them. I shall behave like an amateur. But why should you run any risk?

MAZZINI: Think of the risk those poor fellows up there are running!

NURSE GUINNESS: Think of them, indeed, the murdering black-guards! What next?

(A terrific explosion shakes the earth. They reel back into their seats, or clutch the nearest support. They hear the falling of the shattered glass from the windows.)

MAZZINI: Is anyone hurt?

HECTOR: Where did it fall?

NURSE GUINNESS: *(In hideous triumph.)* Right in the gravel pit: I seen it. Serve un right! I seen it. *(She runs away toward the gravel pit, laughing harshly.)*

HECTOR: One husband gone.

CAPTAIN SHOTOVER: Thirty pounds of good dynamite wasted.

MAZZINI: Oh, poor Mangan!

HECTOR: Are you immortal that you need pity him? Our turn next.

(They wait in silence and intense expectation. Hesione and Ellie hold each other's hand tight.)

(A distant explosion is heard.)

MRS. HUSHABYE: *(Relaxing her grip.)* Oh! they have passed us.

LADY UTTERWORD: The danger is over, Randall. Go to bed.

CAPTAIN SHOTOVER: Turn in, all hands. The ship is safe. *(He sits down and goes asleep.)*

ELLIE: *(Disappointedly.)* Safe!

HECTOR: *(Disgustedly.)* Yes, safe. And how damnably dull the world has become again suddenly! *(He sits down.)*

MAZZINI: *(Sitting down.)* I was quite wrong, after all. It is we who have survived; and Mangan and the burglar —

HECTOR: — the two burglars —

LADY UTTERWORD: — the two practical men of business —

MAZZINI: — both gone. And the poor clergyman will have to get a new house.

MRS. HUSHABYE: But what a glorious experience! I hope they'll come again tomorrow night.

ELLIE: *(Radiant at the prospect.)* Oh, I hope so.

(Randall at last succeeds in keeping the home fires burning on his flute.)

****

Shaw

THE READING ROOM

YOUNG STUDENTS AND THEIR TEACHERS

Ganz, Arthur F. *George Bernard Shaw*. New York: Grove Press, 1983.

Henderson, Archibald. *George Bernard Shaw: His Life and Works*. London: Hurst and Blackett, 1911.

———. *George Bernard Shaw: Man of the Century*. New York: Appleton-Century-Crofts, 1956.

Kronenberger, Louis. *George Bernard Shaw: A Critical Survey*. Cleveland, Ohio: WorldPublishing, 1953.

Minney, R. J. *Recollections of George Bernard Shaw*. Englewood Cliffs, N.J.: Prentice-Hall, 1969.

West, Alick. *George Bernard Shaw: "a good man fallen among Fabians."* New York: International Publishers, 1950.

SCHOLARS, STUDENTS, PROFESSORS

Adams, Elsie B. *Bernard Shaw and the Aesthetes*. Columbus: Ohio State University Press, 1971.

———, ed. *Critical Essays on George Bernard Shaw*. New York: Maxwell Macmillian International, 1991.

Bloom, Harold, ed. *George Bernard Shaw's Man and Superman*. New York: Chelsea House, 1987.

———. *The Literary Criticism of John Ruskin*. New York: Da Capo Press, 1987.

Casteras, Susan P., et al. *John Ruskin and the Victorian Eye*. New York: Harry N. Abrams, 1993.

Chesterton, G. K. *George Bernard Shaw*. New York: John Lane, 1914.

Craig, David M. *John Ruskin and the Ethics of Consumption*. Charlottesville: University of Virginia Press, 2006.

Hill, E. C. *George Bernard Shaw*. Boston: Twayne Publishers, 1978.

This extensive bibliography lists books about the playwright according to whom the books might be of interest. If you would like to research further something that interests you in the text, lists of references, sources cited, and editions used in this book are found in this section.

Innes, Christopher, ed. *The Cambridge Companion to George Bernard Shaw*. New York: Cambridge University Press, 1998.

Morgan, Hilary, and Peter Nahum. *Burne-Jones, the Pre-Raphaelites and Their Century*. London: Peter Nahum, 1989.

Morris, William, et al. *Hand and Brain: A Symposium of Essays on Socialism*. Aurora, N.Y.: Roycrofters at the Roycroft Shop, 1898.

Pater, Walter. *Walter Pater: Three Major Texts (The Renaissance, Appreciations, and Imaginary Portraits)*. William E. Buckler, ed. New York: New York University Press, 1986.

Prettejohn, Elizabeth, ed. *After the Pre-Raphaelites: Art and Aestheticism in Victorian England*. New Brunswick, N.J.: Rutgers University Press, 1999.

———. *The Art of the Pre-Raphaelites*. London: Tate Publishing, 2000.

Richards, Shaun. *The Cambridge Companion to Twentieth-Century Irish Drama*. Cambridge: Cambridge University Press, 2004.

Shaw, George Bernard. *Essays in Fabian Socialism*. London: Constable, 1932.

———. *The Adventures of the Black Girl in Her Search for God*. London: Constable, 1933

THEATERS, PRODUCERS

Dent, Alan, ed. *Bernard Shaw and Mrs. Patrick Campbell: Their Correspondence*. New York: Knopf, 1952.

Henderson, Archibald. *Bernard Shaw: Playboy and Prophet*. New York: D. Appleton, 1932.

Hyde, Mary, ed. *Bernard Shaw and Alfred Douglas: A Correspondence*. New Haven, Conn.: Ticknor & Fields, 1982.

Lathem, Edward Connery, ed. *George Bernard Shaw: Eight Interviews*. Peacham, Vt.: Perpetua Press, 2002.

Peters, Sally. *Bernard Shaw: The Ascent of the Superman*. New Haven, Conn.: Yale University Press, 1996.

ACTORS, DIRECTORS, PROFESSIONALS

Berst, Charles A. *Bernard Shaw and the Art of Drama*. Urbana: University of Illinois Press, 1973.

Davis, Tracy C. *George Bernard Shaw and the Socialist Theatre*. Westport, Conn.: Praeger Publishers, 1994.

Garebian, Keith. *George Bernard Shaw and Christopher Newton: Explorations of Shavian Theatre*. Oakville, Ontario: Mosaic Press, 1993.

Jackson, Allan Stuart. *The Standard Theatre of Victorian England*. Rutherford, N.J.: Fairleigh Dickinson University Press, 1993

Jackson, Russell, ed. *Victorian Theatre: The Theatre in Its Time*. New York: New Amsterdam, 1989.

Kaye, Julian B. *Bernard Shaw and the Nineteenth-Century Tradition*. Norman: University of Oklahoma Press, 1958.

Mander, Raymond, and Joe Mitchenson. *Theatrical Companion to Shaw: A Pictorial Record of the First Performances of the Plays of George Bernard Shaw*. New York: Pitman, 1955.

Matthews, John F. *George Bernard Shaw*. New York: Columbia University Press, 1969.

Mencken, H. L. *George Bernard Shaw: His Plays*. Boston and London: J. W. Luce & Co., 1905.

Nicoll, Allardyce. *A History of Late Nineteenth-Century Drama, 1850–1900*. Cambridge: Cambridge University Press, 1946.

Pagliaro, Harold. *Relations Between the Sexes in the Plays of George Bernard Shaw*. Lewiston, N.Y.: Edwin Mellen Press, 2004.

Peters, Margot. *Bernard Shaw and the Actresses*. Garden City, N.Y.: Doubleday, 1980.

Shaw, George Bernard. *The Admirable Bashville; Or, Constancy Unrewarded*. New York: Brentano's, 1907.

———. *You Never Can Tell: A Comedy in Four Acts*. Boston: C. Schellenberg, 1909.

———. *Back to Methuselah: A Metabiological Pentateuch*. New York: Brentano's, 1929.

———. *George Bernard Shaw's Plays*. Edited by Sandie Byrne. New York: W. W. Norton, 2002.

Woodbridge, Homer E. *George Bernard Shaw: Creative Artist*. Carbondale: Southern Illinois University Press, 1963.

EDITIONS OF SHAW'S WORK USED FOR THIS BOOK

Shaw's plays are in the public domain. The excerpts used in Dramatic Moments from the Major Plays are from the following Web sites:

Man and Superman: www.bartleby.com/157/

Major Barbara: http://drama.eserver.org/plays/modern/major-barbara/index_html

Pygmalion: www.gutenberg.org/dirs/3/8/2/3825/3825.txt

Heartbreak House: www.gutenberg.org/dirs/3/5/4/3543/3543.txt

SOURCES CITED IN THIS BOOK

Bax, Clifford, ed. *Florence Farr, Bernard Shaw and W. B. Yeats; Letters.* London: Home & Van Thal, 1946.

Bentley, Eric. *Bernard Shaw.* New York: Applause Theatre & Cinema Books, 2002.

Dervin, Daniel. *Bernard Shaw: A Psychological Study.* Lewisburg, Penn.: Bucknell University Press, 1975.

Holroyd, Michael. *Bernard Shaw: The One-Volume Definitive Edition.* London: Chatto & Windus, 1997.

Laurence, Dan H., and Peters, Margot, eds. *Unpublished Shaw*, vol. 16. University Park: Pennsylvania State University Press, 1996.

Raby, P., ed. *The Cambridge Companion to Oscar Wilde.* Cambridge: Cambridge University Press, 1997.

Shaw, George Bernard. *Plays Pleasant and Unpleasant.* Chicago and New York: Herbert Stone & Co, 1898.

———. *The Quintessence of Ibsenism.* London: W. Scott, 1891.

———. *Immaturity.* London: Constable and Company, 1931.

———. *The Simpleton of the Unexpected Isles, The Six of Calais and The Millionaires: Three Plays by Bernard Shaw.* New York: Dodd, Mead & Company, 1936.

Weintraub, Stanley. *Bernard Shaw: The Diaries, 1885–1897,* vols. I and II. University Park: Pennsylvania State University Press, 1986.

Awards

"And the winner is . . . "

GEORGE BERNARD SHAW HONORS AND AWARDS

1925 Nobel Prize in Literature

1939 Oscar for Best Writing (Adapted Screenplay) for *Pygmalion*,
   shared with Ian Dalrymple, Cecil Lewis, and W. P. Lipscomb.

| | PULITZER PRIZE | TONY AWARD | NY DRAMA CRITICS CIRCLE AWARD | | |
			Best American	Best Foreign	Best Play
1918	Jesse Lynch Williams *Why Marry?*	—	—		
1919	No Award	—	—		
1920	Eugene O'Neill *Beyond the Horizon*	—	—		
1921	Zona Gale *Miss Lulu Bett*	—	—		
1922	Eugene O'Neill *Anna Christie*	—	—		
1923	Owen Davis *Icebound*	—	—		
1924	Hatcher Hughes *Hell-Bent Fer Heaven*	—	—		
1925	Sidney Howard *They Knew What They Wanted*	—	—		

This awards chart is provided for reference so you can see who was winning the major writing awards during the writing career of the playwright.

INDEX

The entries in the index include highlights from the main In an Hour essay portion of the book.

89

ABOUT THE AUTHOR

Emily Esfahani Smith, a graduate of Dartmouth College, is a journalist and writer in Washington, D.C. Her work on cultural, political, and international affairs has appeared in *The Wall Street Journal*, *The Weekly Standard*, *National Review*, *The American Spectator*, and *The New Criterion*.

Know the playwright, love the play.

Open a new door to theater study, performance, and audience satisfaction with these Playwrights In an Hour titles.

ANCIENT GREEK

Aeschylus   Aristophanes   Euripides   Sophocles

RENAISSANCE

William Shakespeare

MODERN

Anton Chekhov   Noël Coward   Lorraine Hansberry
Henrik Ibsen   Arthur Miller   Molière   Eugene O'Neill
Arthur Schnitzler   George Bernard Shaw   August Strindberg
Frank Wedekind   Oscar Wilde   Thornton Wilder
Tennessee Williams

CONTEMPORARY

Edward Albee   Alan Ayckbourn   Samuel Beckett
Theresa Rebeck   Sarah Ruhl   Sam Shepard   Tom Stoppard
August Wilson

To purchase or for more information
visit our web site inanhourbooks.com